Policing a Perplexed Society

Policing a Perplexed Society

by

Sir Robert Mark
Commissioner of Police of the Metropolis

London
GEORGE ALLEN & UNWIN LTD
Ruskin House   Museum Street

First published in 1977
Second impression 1977

ISBN 0 04 363005 7 hardback
     0 04 363006 5 paperback

Printed in Great Britain
by William Clowes & Sons, Ltd.
London, Beccles and Colchester

Preface

It would be undesirable for the Commissioner of Police of the Metropolis to sit down and write a book. What follows is a selection of papers delivered in the course of duty to different audiences and for different purposes, but carefully chosen to present a consistent view of the role of the police in modern society and of its limitations. They have been worked over for publication, but each carries the label of its origin, although figures have generally been updated.

They are published because in my view the effectiveness of the force largely depends on public goodwill and this in turn largely rests on public understanding. The police in this country have nothing to lose and everything to gain by offering the fullest possible account of their activities. Trust begets trust. And the police are the most accurate reflection of British society: they are the visible representation of government by consent, with all the limitations that imposes. They must provide a stabilising and reassuring influence in a changing and often perplexed society. The reader will discern that in my view the police function is one of the most worthwhile in a free society; that we have no cause for shame; and incidentally that I am not one of those who regard this country as passing through a period of unrelieved decadence.

These addresses have been collected for the convenience of those who wish to read them in full and at leisure. The author's receipts from their sale go to the Police Dependants' Trust.

RM
New Scotland Yard

Contents

1
Cornerstones of Excellence*

One of the most frequent comments by visitors to Great Britain is that our policemen are wonderful. It has, perhaps, become less common of late because policemen everywhere are being looked at more critically as their role in free societies becomes more difficult. But in Britain at least, that sentiment continues to be expressed from time to time and not always by visitors from abroad. Three independent public opinion polls in the last eighteen months suggest that the police enjoy more confidence and respect than any other British institution. Oddly enough, most of those who make approving comments about the police would not, if pressed, be able to find convincing reasons for their view. I think most of them would rely on the general impression of a comparatively orderly society, the fact that police do not carry firearms as a routine measure and seem able to control political demonstrations and industrial disputes without using any special weapons or equipment and not least our constant and frequently seen readiness to help anyone in distress or to respond to public need in any kind of emergency. These factors undoubtedly make a deep impression on public opinion, but they are really only superficial indications of a relationship determined by much more significant realities, of which the predominant are, firstly, the limitation of police powers, secondly, our high degree of

* Delivered to the Police Foundation, Washington, USA, in April 1976.

accountability for our actions and thirdly, our freedom from political interference in operational matters at any level, central or local.

It is these factors above all which determine public confidence because they ensure that the police reflect society as a whole. We discharge the communal will, not that of any government minister, mayor or other public official, or that of any political party, whilst remaining fully accountable to the community for what we do or fail to do. And our constitutional freedom facilitates the discharge of the most important of our many duties, the preservation of individual freedom under the law, including the freedom of minorities to express views likely to provoke active public dissent.

There is a fourth factor, more general but no less important, which necessarily governs our effectiveness and reputation, namely, the acceptability of the laws we are required to enforce. But I will deal with that later.

It is often said that the liberties of which Englishmen are rightly proud are rooted in the supremacy of Parliament and the independence of the courts from the executive or government. Perfectly true. But those roots would not go very deep without a police force willing and determined to ensure that the rulings of Parliament and the courts are observed; a task sometimes requiring courage, both moral and physical. Before the establishment of professional police forces in the nineteenth century, those rulings were sometimes treated with scant respect. The enjoyment of liberty and safety under the law was then too often dependent on personal courage or resources. In June 1780 at the most dangerous moment of the American War of Independence Londoners were more concerned with what seemed to them a sea of flames destroying their own City. During the Anti-Popery Gordon Riots which lasted about a week, Newgate and the Fleet Prisons were sacked and the prisoners liberated as were those in Clerkenwell and New Prisons, an orgy of looting, destruction and fire brought London to a standstill. Two hundred and ten people were killed outright and seventy-five more died in hospital. Of four hundred and fifty people arrested, sixty-two were sentenced to death, twenty-five being eventually hanged. That outbreaks of this kind are unthinkable today is entirely due to the police. It is perhaps ironical that of all public services we are the most taken for granted and the least understood. I doubt whether one in a thousand Englishmen could give even a vague outline of our organisation, accountability or method of control. This is a pity because the English police system, reconciling as it does the conflicting aims of preserving individual freedom with the duty of the state to protect itself and its citizens, is undoubtedly one of the most sophisticated and successful institutions to emerge from the English way of life.

There are about 106,000 police (of whom nearly 6,000 are women) in England and Wales, roughly one for every 450 citizens. We are unarmed, although firearms are available to a comparatively small number of specially trained men in emergencies. It needs only a little reflection on those numbers to appreciate that to some extent the term 'police force' is misleading, since our tradition is to achieve our objectives by the avoidance of force, if at all possible. The use of force by policemen in Great Britain is necessarily qualified by the need for its approval or acceptance by the people and by the courts. If that acceptance is not forthcoming the use of force must rebound upon the police themselves, both personally and collectively, because individually we are answerable to the law just like any other citizen. If we exceed our powers we can be prosecuted or sued and if a citizen suffers wrong from a policeman who cannot be identified his chief officer can be found liable for that wrongdoing. We are taught at the outset of our police careers that obedience to orders affords no defence for wrongdoing or misuse of authority.

In theory, responsibility for enforcing the law in Great Britain has always been local. Apart from a brief period under Oliver Cromwell there has never been a national organisation charged with that responsibility. Each citizen is still in theory responsible for enforcing the laws made by his elected representatives in Parliament. He can himself institute prosecutions in England and Wales, though not in Scotland, and he must respond to a call for assistance by a police officer. But, of course, in practice it does not work like that. One of the requirements of an overcrowded, industrialised society is for professional, highly trained police-men to discharge that duty on behalf of their fellow citizens. But, apart from a few exceptions determined by Parliament, the individual police officer in England and Wales still retains the inherent right of every citizen to initiate pro-ceedings against anyone. This is in contrast to the position in Scotland, where authority to prosecute is not exercised by police but by public prosecutors known as procurators fiscal – a system not unlike the American, except that the fiscals are non-elective.

The 106,000 police officers in England and Wales clearly cannot operate effectively in isolation from each other. There is a clear need for organisation, administration and control. The achievement of this without violation of the basic principle of personal responsibility for law enforcement is a classic example of the English genius for compromise. Since the middle of the nineteenth century the police have been attached, for administrative and financial purposes only, to the system of local government, the central government paying half the cost in return for compliance with Regula-tions designed to ensure uniformity in every aspect of police organisation and administration. This means, in effect, that the responsibility for policing rests upon a threefold partner-ship between central government, local government and the police themselves. The result is a system which looks like a national service but which, in fact, in England and Wales comprises forty-three separate, autonomous but closely related forces governed by identical conditions of service including common rates of pay and pension and sharing many common services to achieve greater efficiency. Let us now look briefly at the division of responsibility between the three partners.

The forces outside London vary in size from roughly 700 to 7,000. Each is commanded by a chief officer, a professional policeman chosen by the police authority, a term which I will explain in a moment. The chief officer is the promotion and disciplinary authority for all but the most senior ranks and he exercises the right of appointment to the force. His control of the force is, however, subject to the Regulations I mentioned. These are made by the Home Secretary who is a senior government minister, after consultation with the Police Council, a national body on which police authorities and the police themselves are all represented. The Regulations govern almost every aspect of police administration, for example, pay, promotion, discipline and pensions, and compliance with them is a condition of a government contribution of half of the cost of the force initially borne by the local taxpayer.

The police authority for the Metropolitan Police is the Home Secretary. In the other forces it is a committee of elected local government representatives and magistrates in the proportion of two to one. Appointment to the magistracy, by the way, is by the head of the judiciary, the Lord Chancellor. The duties of the police authority include appointing the chief officer, his deputy and assistants, and if necessary, calling upon them to retire in the interests of efficiency, fixing the establishment of the force and paying for its upkeep out of local taxes and providing buildings and equipment. Individual members of police authorities have no responsibility for the enforcement of law in particular cases but they have an overall if rather tenuous responsibility for the efficiency of the force and for satisfying themselves about the number of complaints against the police and the manner in which they are dealt with.

The Home Secretary has wide powers over both chief officers and police authorities. Appointments to senior posts are subject to his approval and appeals against disciplinary punishments go to him. He is empowered to demand reports from chief officers on any matter and he can institute inquiries into the administration of a police force by any person he chooses. He can require a police authority to retire its chief officer, and on his satisfaction with the efficiency of the force depends the annual refund by the government of half its expenditure.

In fact, however, coercive powers are rarely, if ever, used. The forty-three forces operate harmoniously under the threefold partnership of the police, police authorities and the Home Office. There are three police staff associations or unions which meet regularly to discuss professional and domestic matters, the police authorities having similar arrangements. All three, police, police authorities and Home Office, are represented on joint negotiating bodies on whose advice the Home Secretary issues the Regulations governing the administration of the service and which, amongst other things, require forces to aid each other in emergencies.

The achievement of uniform standards of organisation and efficiency by financial inducement has made it possible to transform the police service in England and Wales from a rather mixed collection of some 200 forces, as recently as 1945, many of them inward looking and subject to improper local influence, to the present network of forty-three forces, all enjoying the exclusive right of law enforcement within their own areas but observing common standards demo-cratically negotiated and thus presenting the appearance of a national force whilst retaining the advantages of local autonomy, flexibility and accountability. This has facilitated the emergence of what we call common services, or ac-tivities which we can better undertake jointly than separ-ately. The training of recruits, for example, is done at a small number of district training centres, each serving a number of forces by which they are administered.

Regional crime squads provide a national detective net-work directed against target criminals and working in close collaboration with the police forces from which their mem-bers are drawn and to which they will return after temporary secondment for a few years. Forensic science laboratories and regional wireless depots similarly serve the whole country under the aegis of the Home Office, which is also developing computerisation on a national scale. One of the most im-portant common services is the National Police College at Bramshill. This was established in 1948 to raise the standards of efficiency throughout the police service and to provide the future leaders of the service.

It was Sir Robert Peel's intention that the police service should find its own leaders but between 1829 when the

Metropolitan force was established and 1948, it had shown itself largely incapable of doing so. About a quarter of appointments to the highest rank had been made from outside the police, in particular from the armed forces. The purpose of the College was primarily, therefore, to enable the police service to afford higher training facilities for all forces, to identify and develop the young officer with exceptional intellectual and command potential, to improve and spread professional knowledge and, not least important, to broaden the experience and outlook of those destined for intermediate and senior command.

The College is controlled by a board of governors consisting of senior civil servants, chief officers of police and representatives from local government and the police staff associations or unions.

There is an ascending scale of courses. At the lowest level, the special course of one year trains young constables of outstanding promise who have been selected by an extended interview on a national basis. It is possible for an officer to qualify for this course before the end of his third year of service. Standards for admission are very high and each year only thirty to forty applicants are accepted. Successful completion assures immediate promotion to sergeant and after one year's satisfactory service in that rank further promotion to inspector.

The largest course is that for recently promoted inspectors. It lasts three months. Selection is made by chief officers according to a quota of places based on the strength of each force and 140 inspectors from the forty-three forces are in training at any one time.

Four overseas command courses, each of three months, are held each year. These are designed to train senior officers of overseas police forces for the responsibilities of assistant commissioner and above. Generally speaking the students are drawn from countries who are members of the British Commonwealth.

At the upper end of the scale, command training for senior officers is undertaken in two parts. The first provides training for forty-five superintendents on four three-month courses to equip them for divisional or departmental command and is an essential preliminary to the second part which is designed to equip even more senior officers for ultimate command.

The content of all College courses includes a substantial element of liberal studies. The College has never been restricted to the narrow professional field of criminal law and police procedure. It was felt essential that police officers should understand and be able to communicate with and to manage their fellow men; that they should be able to enforce the law and still maintain a human relationship with the public. A wide range of academic studies is, therefore, provided by seventeen full-time tutors who are graduates in philosophy, politics, economics, English, psychology, sociology and management studies.

At command-course level some emphasis is laid on acquiring an understanding of modern managerial attitudes and methods and some familiarity with scientific and technological apparatus, particularly computers which are increasingly being brought into use not only for administrative purposes but for command and control of operational deployment. To counter any danger of insularity, students spend a week in other European countries examining pre-selected problems in the fields of crime, traffic and public order. A further valuable contribution to the extension of their experience is the presence on the course of a number of officers from other countries. These have included officers from the United States including the FBI, Europe, West Indies, the Middle East and Australasia.

In 1964 a scheme to produce our own university graduates from within the service by sending the most able students from the special and inspectors' courses to university was introduced to counter the apparent lack of attraction of a police career for university graduates generally.

This scheme, in which the College nominates candidates for scholarships to universities subject to the approval of their chief officers and police authorities, enables officers usually of the rank of inspector to take a degree of their choice, usually in law, social sciences, psychology, administrative sciences or combined subjects. During their three years at university they receive their full pay and allowances and no conditions are imposed about their future service with the police.

The Police College scholars' success in university examinations, and their participation in university life, have been impressive. The great majority achieve good honours degrees and wastage is very small. This scheme provides an unequalled opportunity for contact between some of the best young officers of the service and those who will eventually occupy influential positions in the community.

Perhaps the most important effect of the College has been the emergence of a unity of philosophy and purpose within the service. The bringing together of officers of varied professional backgrounds to learn, to discuss and to exchange experience has been instrumental not only in forging valuable, personal inter-force links but in the acceptance of the concept of a police service by those whose horizons have hitherto been restricted to their own force boundaries.

The authority of each police officer extends to the whole of England and Wales. Interchange between the forty-three forces, with retention of pay and pension rights, is common and for those aspiring to the highest ranks, obligatory. Every chief officer must, therefore, have served in two or more forces before being appointed. Graduation from the senior command course at the College is inevitably and rightly coming to be regarded as an essential qualification for those aiming at chief officer rank.

The cumulative effect of the amalgamation of police forces into fewer and more efficient units, of steadily increasing uniformity of organisation, methods and standards, the increasing extent of common services including computerisation and, perhaps most important of all, the enlightening and uplifting role of the National Police College, is the emergence of the British police as a unified service having a stabilising and reassuring influence in an inevitably changing and uncertain society. We are no longer just the shock absorber, or the oil which lessens the frictions of society. We are now the bastion to which people at every level look for reassurance and comfort.

The emergence of a unified yet local service enjoying a high degree of public confidence is encouraging, but it is not enough. You will recall that I mentioned a fourth factor determining our relationship with the people – the acceptability of the laws we are required to enforce. No matter how efficient and accountable the police, we are only one part of the process that we call criminal justice. The making of laws, the rules for investigating wrongdoing and trying offenders, the treatment of the accused and the guilty, all these are part of that process, and widespread public ignorance tends to lay upon the police the blame for the failure of any one of them. If laws are unenforceable, or only enforceable sporadically, and therefore unfairly, people blame the police, not the legislature. If the balance of the criminal process is weighted too heavily on the side of the suspected or accused person the police cannot be effective. In a free society people find that it attracts more votes or popularity to challenge the validity of a conviction or the denial of bail than to question the acquittal of the guilty, which is no less a miscarriage of justice, or to analyse the effects of too-liberal bail procedures. It is important also to understand that no one but the police sees collectively the failure of the criminal process. We alone know the numbers of crimes not followed by prosecution of the offender, of crimes committed on bail, of acquittals of those who are only too obviously not innocent. We alone experience the collective effect of the difference between the theory of criminal justice and its defects in practice, which undermines its efficiency and lessens public confidence in it. In Britain the police are coming to realise that the public interest requires us to gather and make known information of this kind to the public itself rather than to those who have vested interests in the making or practice of law. There are, of course, great difficulties. The laws of libel, of privilege and contempt prevent us from exposing the worst failures of the criminal process, but gradually we are acquiring the technique of drawing public attention to evidence showing systematic weaknesses or failure, rather than of individual instances of malpractice or injustice. By this means we persuaded the government in 1967 to abandon unanimous jury verdicts in criminal trials and to require also the pre-trial disclosure of alibi defences. One in every eight or nine findings of guilt these days is by a majority of not less than ten to two. The enormous saving in time and money by the avoidance of re-trials has not been countered by any expression of public or judicial disquiet or dissatisfaction.

We hope before the end of this century, if not this decade, to persuade the government to abolish the caution against self-incrimination and to require the accused to enter the witness box to speak or remain silent, as he pleases, the intention being, of course, that the credibility of the accused should relate at least to some extent to his spontaneity rather than to the period of silence between arrest and trial which has produced, and continues to produce, some of the most predictable, ingenious and highly paid fiction of our time.

There is, I think, a price that we in Great Britain must pay for public acceptance of changes of this kind. We must first accept that no punishment by criminal process should be irrevocable. In other words, the death penalty should not be restored. Second, we must be willing to accept a high degree of supervision of and accountability for our own handling of criminal cases and of complaints. This willingness must extend to the establishment of machinery and procedures for dealing effectively with complaints of police wrongdoing and corruption, coupled with continuing revision of administrative selection and promotion procedures, so as to make wrongdoing less likely and more certain of detection and punishment if and when it does occur. We have made extensive progress along these lines during the last few years in London, and are presently discussing with the government a review of our complaints procedure.

As a professional policeman in my thirty-ninth year of service, I believe that the best deterrent to deliberate and therefore preventable crime is not the severity of punishment unlikely to be applied, but the probability of detection, or being caught, followed by the near certainty of conviction of the guilty. I do not, of course, imply that the protection of society may not require the imposition of imprisonment for life, but certainly in Britain the number of cases involving that requirement is comparatively small. The cornerstone of my belief is that the purpose of criminal justice should not, as at present, be the establishment of technical guilt as a prerequisite to punishment, but the discovery of the truth, without which it seems to me unreasonable to expect justice to be effective or to command public confidence. Some of you may think that as policemen it is improper for you to comment on general terms on the process of justice, that your purpose should be confined to administering a system devised by others. That was certainly so in Britain, but we have come to realise that the police have a duty to contribute from their experience to public discussion of the purposes and procedures of criminal justice. We know as much about it as anyone, and exclusion from public debate about its strengths and weaknesses must inevitably detract from our status and discourage recruitment and retention of the sort of men necessary to create and maintain the kind of service that both police and public really want. Whatever one hears or reads about the economic or other problems of Great Britain, in the sphere of policing we regard ourselves as being in excellent health and likely to be widely regarded in the fairly near future as one of the most important and beneficial influences upon English social life. Our problems, like yours, are great, but our morale and, I like to think, our reputation have never been higher.

2

Keeping the Peace in Great Britain: The Differing Roles of the Police and the Army*

Notwithstanding your kindness in conferring an honorary degree upon me, some ten years ago, I am not really learned in the law and I am not in the academic sense a man of letters. I do, however, have one commodity of interest to universities and indeed to society generally; a knowledge of the theory and practice of police administration and operations of which virtually no information is readily available to the public or even to the social historian. I would, therefore, like to take this opportunity to shed some light on a subject about which needless secrecy or reserve is more likely to provoke than allay social disquiet, and on which I think a little plain speaking is long overdue, namely, the extent to which there is, and ought to be, contingency planning between the police and the army in Great Britain for certain limited purposes not involving any threat to, or diminution of, civil liberty.

I propose to begin by asserting that within Great Britain the police represent government by consent. We are very

* Delivered to the Convocation of Leicester University in March 1976.

few in number and we are for the most part unarmed. We live among the communities we serve and our mobility is necessarily limited. Our authority under the law is strictly defined and we are personally liable for the consequences whenever we invoke it. We play no part in determining guilt or punishment and our accountability to the courts both criminal and civil, to local police authorities, to Parliament and to public opinion is unsurpassed anywhere else in the world. In the legal and constitutional framework in which society requires us to enforce the laws enacted by its elected representatives, the most essential weapons in our armoury are not firearms, water cannon, tear gas or rubber bullets, but the confidence and support of the people on whose behalf we act. That confidence and support depends not only on the factors I have already mentioned but on our personal and collective integrity and in particular on our long tradition of constitutional freedom from political interference in our operational role. Notwithstanding the heavy responsibilities for the policing of England and Wales given to the Home Secretary by the 1964 Police Act, it is important for you to understand that the police are not the servants of the government at any level. We do not act at the behest of a minister or any political party, not even the party in government. We act on behalf of the people as a whole and the powers we exercise cannot be restricted or widened by anyone, save Parliament alone. It is this which above all else determines our relationship with the public, especially in relation to the maintenance of public order, and allows us to operate reasonably effectively with minimal numbers, limited powers and by the avoidance of force, or at least with the use only of such force as will be approved by the courts and by public opinion. It is of course true that the Prosecution of Offences Act and Regulations enable the Director of Public Prosecutions to initiate and control police inquiries and prosecutions, but he is accountable to Parliament through the Attorney General, and those powers are not relevant to operational police decisions in dealing with matters of public order. (Rather different considerations apply in Scotland where prosecutions are undertaken by

procurators fiscal appointed by the Lord Advocate.) To sum
the position up for you in easily understandable and practical
terms, a chief officer of police will always give the most
careful consideration to any views or representations he may
receive from his police authority, be it Home Secretary or
police committee, on any issue affecting enforcement of the
law, whether public order or anything else, but in England
and Wales it is generally for him and him alone to decide
what operational action to take and to answer for the
consequences. In the case of the Commissioner of Police of
the Metropolis his exercise of those responsibilities will no
doubt be all the more scrupulous in that he alone of all
chief police officers enjoys no security of tenure and that
subject to parliamentary approval he may be removed by
the Home Secretary. A provincial chief officer may be
retired by his police authority with the consent, or on the
direction, of the Home Secretary in the interests of efficiency,
but he is entitled to an inquiry by one or more persons
appointed by the Home Secretary before suffering that fate.

I emphasise this because whilst the police place great
importance on their constitutional freedom the significance of
their accountability should not be overlooked as a counterbalance to any improper use of it. Our role, therefore, is that
of keeping the peace by the use of old, complex and sensitive
procedures and machinery whereby in a democratic society
lawlessness is contained and excesses are controlled by
methods acceptable to the public as a whole. The laws, the
courts, the organs of public opinion, our small numbers and
above all the limitation of our authority and accountability
under the law all contribute to ensure that we are always
the servants rather than the masters of the public. That is
what I meant when I said that we are in fact the visible
manifestation of government by consent.

Now let us consider briefly the rather different role of the
army. The soldier, in contrast to the policeman, is the em-
bodiment of the ultimate sanction of force which is necessary
to every government, even the most democratic, for protection from external attack or for dealing with revolutionary
activities for which the machinery of government by consent

is inadequate. A minority which attempts by armed force to prevent government by consent or to usurp the function of government is engaging in revolutionary activity, no matter what euphemisms it employs to describe its activities. If that minority is sufficiently large, sooner or later it will be necessary to decide whether the ultimate sanction of force rather than the ordinary democratic process of law is necessary to contain or suppress it. Northern Ireland is a classic example of this and notwithstanding that it is not part of Great Britain I clearly ought not to avoid brief mention of it, because of the long-lasting and close involvement of the army in the police function there. I hope I shall be forgiven by Ulstermen, however, for saying on the authority of Lord Cameron amongst others that the Province has never enjoyed government by consent as the term is understood in Great Britain. Its government has always been drawn from one party, increasingly unacceptable to a steadily growing minority. Its inclusion in the United Kingdom suggests to the uninformed that there is little or no difference in our political and social conditions. Even cursory research will show that this is not so and it is, therefore, important that you should not misunderstand the relationship between police and army in Great Britain because of the different conditions which apply in Northern Ireland. The impossibility of maintaining law and order there by ordinary police methods made it necessary in 1969 in the interests of the Province as a whole to invoke military aid to contain the situation until a generally acceptable political solution is found. But the task of the army there, though that of 'keeping the peace' in a literal sense, ought not to be confused with the role of the police on the mainland. The army's task in Ulster is the suppression or containment of force by force or threat of force, even though the degree of force is the minimum sufficient for the purpose. It does not act, as a police force does, on behalf of the community as a whole, but on the orders of its political masters to whom it is, through its command structure, accountable. The line of command runs from soldier to battalion, brigade, division, corps, army to the CGS, CDS and of course the Minister of

Defence. The ultimate objective of the army is to contain the situation with as little loss of life and destruction of property as possible until return to government by consent permits the resumption of ordinary policing, but it is important to note that the soldier enjoys no immunity from the criminal, civil or military law whilst discharging this duty. It is a thankless task. No one knows better than a policeman the courage and tolerance necessary to stand between opposing extremes so often so unreasonable, and when both sides have recourse to extreme violence the task of containment requires the highest virtues to which man can aspire.

If I may be permitted an aside, never in all its long history has the army better deserved the gratitude and admiration of the nation than during its recent years in Ulster even though its role there lacks the glamour or the glory of the battlefield or the successful campaign of conquest or defence. Even the *Washington Post*, viewing the scene with a transatlantic eye, traditionally sympathetic to the Irish, is of that view. Its correspondent Alfred Friendly wrote in its pages some time ago: 'Except for Catholics in Ulster, the British see their 14,000 man force there as behaving splendidly (as indeed it is) with courage, incredible restraint and discipline in the face of what would have been thought to be intolerable conditions of insult, provocation and huge physical risks. Television, night after terrible night, has shown the army in a most favourable and even inspiring light.' A tribute which the evidence of your own eyes may suggest is richly deserved.

In Great Britain itself the army was used briefly by Cromwell during the Protectorate for police purposes. This was of course long before the establishment of professional police. The scheme was not unlike the deployment of paramilitary police in national socialist Germany. It was unpopular, ineffective and soon abandoned. The army was, thereafter, used intermittently to suppress or contain riots and political demonstrations in the eighteenth and nineteenth centuries and this persisted even after the establishment of the Metropolitan force in 1829, but its occasional use in a police role was always unpopular, sure to arouse public resentment and controversy and steadily diminished as the police increased in numbers and improved in efficiency. The army has not been used in that role in Great Britain since the 1914–18 war. (The army played only a small part in the General Strike of 1926. Naval ratings were used in considerable numbers at the docks and power stations. The RAF provided amongst other things a shuttle service for urgent documents, but the army's role, with one or two exceptions, of which the most notable was the London docks, was passive.) There has thus emerged with the passage of time a firm and deepening conviction, shared by soldiers, police and public alike that the army has no part to play in Great Britain in matters of political and industrial dispute not involving the overthrow of lawful government by force. It is true that there have been occasions in the last half-century and in recent years on which either violence or the extreme pursuit of sectional interests during industrial disputes has prompted widespread comment and apprehension about what is loosely called the rule of law. But such incidents, though sometimes provoking understandable misgiving, have generally been countered by the pendulum of public opinion which can and does tend to swing against those who behave in that way. Political change is inevitable in a shifting, turbulent and competitive society. The only such change that could and should involve any reaction from either police or army is that attempted by violence, in the case of the army protracted violence beyond the capacity of police containment, and that has fortunately not so far been our tradition, at least in this century.

It will not, therefore, surprise you when I tell you that the prospect of invoking military force to deal with industrial disputes or political demonstrations has never been contemplated during my thirty-nine years' service and there are, so far as I know, no plans at all for such a contingency. Having made that clear, perhaps I can be equally frank in telling you that there have always been plans for invoking military aid to help us deal with civil disasters such as floods, rescues and so on and that latterly there has emerged a need for contingency plans for military aid to deal with situations in which defensive armour, sophisticated weaponry and specialised training might minimise loss of life in dealing with armed and dangerous men inspired by political motives; in other words political terrorists as distinct from armed criminals. There is nothing mysterious or disquieting about this. The police, mostly unarmed and never armed for routine duties, have in recent years found it necessary to acquire, with the approval of government and police authorities, a limited number of firearms for protection against armed criminals, including political terrorists who are always likely to be comparatively few in number. The extent of police reaction will always be limited, not merely for reasons of economy and safety, but also because the police themselves generally object to carrying firearms except when really necessary. This development poses no threat at all to civil liberties, no matter what radical extremists may say. We are equipped only to deal with armed criminals and political terrorists not posing any extraordinary problem or capable of posing only a limited threat.

Moreover, in doing so without military aid we retain the right to make our own appreciation, decide our own tactics and take such operational action as we think necessary whilst remaining, each one of us, personally accountable to the law for our actions. In doing so, of course, we will avail ourselves of expert advice and maintain close liaison with other authorities likely to be of help. In the case of the Metropolitan Police close liaison with the Home Office ensures a ready availability of every possible kind of assistance. A police officer armed in such circumstances will always be carefully briefed and in a static situation will be led by senior officers, but in the last resort it is he, and he alone, who will decide whether he is justified in using his firearm to protect himself. He does not need the permission of a senior officer. A jury or a police disciplinary inquiry may examine his actions but his use of a firearm does not differ in law from his use of a truncheon. Clearly, however, dangerous situations may arise which, notwithstanding their training, their willingness and their courage, policemen are less likely to resolve with minimum loss of life than the army.

In such situations, permission of the Home Secretary is sought by the chief officer of police to invoke military aid and the Minister of Defence, in consultation with the Home Secretary, who will have considered the views of the chief officer of police, will decide whether to authorise the ultimate sanction of force by such troops as he may make available. Such assistance was formerly sought by police from the magistracy rather than from the Home Office, but whatever the legal position the present practice reflects the emergence of a professional, well-organised police service which has inevitably assumed the primary responsibility for law and order. The repeal of the Riot Act is perhaps another indication of that trend. The request to the Home Secretary having been approved, it is clearly desirable that both police and the army should then conform to exactly the same terms of engagement. There is no question of one service coming under command of the other. The police commander would simply indicate to the military commander the problem and the target and offer him whatever support he required whilst playing a containing or supporting role. The army commander would act in accordance with the joint police/army plan. He would not be under the command of the police commander but would act in conjunction with him under his duty at common law to come to the aid of the civil power. The joint objective would, of course, be to bring the operation to a successful conclusion, ideally without loss of life. But its achievement would clearly involve a voluntary if temporary, restriction of the right of the police to complete freedom under the law in their operational decisions and actions. In such circumstances police, army, Home Office and Ministry of Defence must act in complete accord.

The army can also be made available through the same channel of communication in a protective and deterrent role in anticipation of armed terrorist activity and as I am sure you will know such operations at Heathrow Airport are now accepted by the public as necessary and sensible.

There is also what I would call, for want of a better word, the logistical role which the army may be called upon to undertake in civil emergencies as, for example, when it shifted a mass of unemptied dustbins during a dustmen's strike at Glasgow. That assistance was not, of course, invoked by the police but by the Glasgow local authority. It was, however, of direct interest to the police, because if the soldiers had met with violence it would have been the task of the police and not the army to deal with it.

It will be obvious from what I have said that military aid to the civil power in Great Britain will always be restricted to very small numbers of troops, strictly limited in purpose and short-lived in duration. This is perhaps just as well in view of the present size of the army and its other commitments.

Perhaps I should complete the picture for you by brief mention of what is called by the press a 'third force' and of 'private armies' which attracted a great deal of comment recently. A 'third force' is an organisation specifically designed for law enforcement thought to be beyond the scope of the civil police but not requiring the sophisticated weaponry and training of the army. Such forces are to be seen in many countries: the National Guard in America, the Bereitschaftspolizei in Berlin, the CRS and Gendarmerie Mobile in France and special units of the Carabinieri in Italy. The Army High Command, the Home Office and the civil police have always been opposed to a third force and believe that the purposes it could achieve are better fulfilled by the police and the army about whose respective roles and accountability there is no ambiguity and who both enjoy public confidence.

The very term 'private army' provokes a vague feeling of apprehension and suggests a fundamental misunderstanding of the problems posed by social or industrial unrest. You cannot control a free society by force, whether by troops, police or private armies or all three. To do so would require very large numbers of men prepared to exercise arbitrary power in the homeland with a ruthlessness required only of soldiers in war. That destroys freedom, as we know it, polarises society and ensures conflict. That is why a government of any democratic party will avoid confrontation between troops and those engaged in civil or industrial disputes.

I must again emphasise by contrast that the use of force by police to maintain public order can never be arbitrary. It is always conditioned by the factors I have briefly outlined to you. We are unarmed, clearly and locally accountable for our actions by legal procedures, well established and widely understood and we are strictly impartial in that we do not act for the government, for any one party or sectional interest. Any need to enlarge national resources to deal with civil disputes will not be lessened by disregard of those fundamental conditions. Such a disregard would increase, not lessen, civil strife. Well-intentioned public concern on this issue should be channelled to strengthen our well-tried and generally accepted institutions rather than to usurp their functions.

I suspect that there may be some among you in whom the title of this lecture aroused curiosity or even faint apprehension, who now feel disappointed by what I have had to say. Occasional references in the news media to the army at London Airport or at Balcombe Street, where armed men were recently besieged, or elsewhere, naturally attract a good deal of interest, speculation and excitement. If indeed some of you do now suffer a sense of anti-climax perhaps you will, on reflection, feel relieved and reassured to know that the task of preserving liberty and maintaining order in this country is still a police function and that the only circumstances in which military aid is likely to be involved are such as to give no cause at all for anxiety or apprehension to those who take it upon themselves to keep a vigilant eye on our civil liberties.

That may be disappointing to radical extremists and political propagandists, but it happens to be true. It is an important part of the police function to act as a shock absorber in protecting society from violence from any source and it is part of our tradition that we do this with the minimal degree of force necessary to deny the violent the achievement of their objectives, whether criminal or political. Do not underestimate the cost in terms of hardship and physical injury. The uniformed branch of some 17,000 men in London suffers about 3,000 assaults each year, three men having to go sick from their injuries every two days. The expectation of physical injury for policemen in London is very high and will remain so, although an increase in manpower for preventive purposes would undoubtedly reduce it.

It is, however, a price we are willing to pay for the preservation of the English way of life. It is all very well for Voltaire to say: 'I disagree with what you say but will defend to the death your right to say it.' In practical terms these days the defence of that right in this country falls to the police, who protect and will continue to protect demonstrators of the extreme right and the extreme left no less than those who march in the face of a hostile crowd to commemorate what they call Bloody Sunday. We, the police, are in fact the most accurate reflection of British society, its tolerance, its strengths and its weaknesses and neither we nor you would welcome or even accept a relinquishment of our role, or any part of it, to the army, other than in the circumstances I have outlined, notwithstanding that both police and army are inspired by the same ideals of service to the people from whom we are drawn and whose well-being is our mutual objective.

3
Liberty without Responsibility ?*

I am not one of those who feel there is, or ought to be, a common bond uniting policemen of all countries. On the contrary, I believe that the police system of each and every country must reflect the society it serves. Each society determines the numbers, the organisation, the powers and the accountability of its police force or police forces and with some of them I desire no more contact than is absolutely necessary.

The authoritarian police forces of totalitarian societies have nothing in common with the police function to which you and I are dedicated, perhaps the most worthwhile and most noble function in any free society. For you and I have this in common, that we represent government by consent. By that I mean that we enforce democratically enacted laws on behalf of the people as a whole and not on behalf of any political party in government or otherwise. There are nevertheless differences in the ways in which we discharge our obligations. Indeed, one of the essential requirements of a truly democratic police system is that whilst adhering to certain basic principles it should be capable of adaptation to meet the requirements of different societies or communities. This is true even of a small island like Great Britain where the English and Welsh have a system quite different from that in

* Address to the Canadian Association of Chiefs of Police, Inc., Toronto, in August 1975, with additions from an Address to the Washington Press Club in April 1976.

Scotland. There are, too, differences between the police of Great Britain and those of other democratic countries, some of which seem to me to afford us a rather unfair advantage when people draw comparisons between us.

We are a small island, able to exercise a reasonably effective control over the entry of people, firearms and drugs. During this century at least we have enjoyed a reasonable degree of prosperity, universal education and, since the last war, an increasing avoidance of poverty of the kind experienced in the thirties. This has encouraged general acceptance of our social system and of the law even by minorities. In the post-war years the state has provided free medical and hospital treatment, generous unemployment benefits, free legal aid for those of low income charged with criminal offences and compensation for people suffering from criminal injuries. Major changes in the law since 1945 have put more emphasis on prevention of crime, the protection of society, the rehabilitation of the offender and the compensation of the victim rather than on punishment as the primary purpose of criminal justice. The legalisation and improved control of betting and gaming, and changing attitudes to prostitution, homosexuality and victimless crime have to a great extent eliminated the aura of corruption which inevitably affected police involved in those matters. This has contributed significantly to an improved police image.

The control of firearms, by which I mean rifles and pistols, is very strict. There are only 24,000 lawfully owned weapons in London with a population of between 7 and 8 million and probably less than half a million in the whole country. Private possession of a firearm is generally regarded as anti-social and unlawful possession is an arrestable offence. The police issue firearms certificates, subject to appeal to the courts against refusal, and we ordinarily only approve ownership for use in rifle and pistol clubs or of trophies or of firearms which have an historical or other interest. Bank guards, security guards, personal bodyguards, private detectives, none of these would have the hope of obtaining a firearm certificate and the penalties for unlawful possession are severe.

There are probably about 2¼ million shotguns, that is smooth-barrelled sporting guns, in Great Britain and these are more commonly used than firearms in robberies and that kind of crime. There were 645 robberies with firearms in 1974, about 7 per cent of the total of 8,666 robberies in that year. Carrying a firearm without lawful authority can attract a five-year prison sentence and if done with intent to injure a person or damage property, life imprisonment. A significant and increasing number of armed robbers are being caught and convicted. Firearms in themselves do not, therefore, pose a serious problem to police even in London and there is not the remotest likelihood of the police arming themselves for routine duties in the foreseeable future. Indeed there would be widespread resistance by the police to such a proposal.

Hand guns, rifles and sophisticated military assistance are all readily available for terrorist or hi-jacking situations, and no other form of weaponry is necessary or contemplated. We believe that our most effective weaponry is the trust and confidence of the communities we serve and the support of the public generally. Another important factor is, I think, that our judiciary at all levels, from the magistrate to the High Court judge, is non-elective and of unquestioned integrity. Perhaps most important of all, however, is that politics play no part at all in the appointment, promotion and operational control of the police generally. It is true that the chief officers and their deputies are appointed by local police committees, but professional experience and the approval of the Home Secretary are necessary. Once appointed they enjoy a virtually unique freedom from political interference in their operational decisions and a high degree of security of tenure. We are fortunate too in our small number of police forces closely linked by identical standards of training, equipment, and so on and sharing such facilities as forensic science laboratories, regional crime squads, criminal records, specialised detection work directed against target criminals, wireless, computers, recruitment and higher training. Half of their expenditure is repaid to local police authorities by the central government subject to certain conditions which include annual inspection by the central government and a requirement to lend each other mutual aid in emergencies.

As I have said elsewhere, it is common and indeed advantageous for officers to have served in more than one force and obligatory for those seeking promotion to the highest ranks. Post-war legislation has eased our task by eliminating many of the former temptations to petty corruption through the reform of laws relating to street betting, gaming and homosexuality. A more tolerant public reaction to licensing, prostitution, plays, cinematograph films and controversial literature has also tended to ease our relationship with the public. My fundamental belief, however, is that the reputation of a police force basically depends on its acceptability and this can only be achieved by a carefully balanced limitation of its powers which allows it to be effective but subject coincidentally to a high degree of accountability to the courts, to its police authority and to the public. This balance is essential to ensure confidence in its integrity and its management. Assuming that in our two countries we share the same objectives for the police in preventing and detecting crime, their attainment involves a number of checks and balances, some of which are controversial. The most important of these are the rules and procedures which govern the investigation of crime and the trial of criminal issues.

I have been a professional policeman now for more than 39 years and only in the last decade have I come to believe that the objective of criminal justice should be the establishment of the truth rather than the technical determination of guilt, which is its present restricted purpose in both our countries. In other words, I think the best deterrent to crime is the likelihood of detection followed by the certainty of conviction, rather than reliance on savage penalties unlikely to be applied in many cases because a proper finding of guilt is prevented by the operation during investigation and trial of safeguards rightly designed to protect the innocent from a sentence of death. This is, of course, an example of my belief that policing and justice must to some extent be influenced by the social, political and other conditions in which we live.

In England and Wales in 1975, for example, the total of homicides (that is murder, manslaughter and infanticide) numbered 600 in relation to 49 million people. The number of policemen murdered on duty during the last decade in the whole country averages between one and two a year as compared with the 947 killed in the United States in the decade 1965/74. Some people perhaps think of us as a country distracted by bombs and terrorist incidents. In fact from March 1973, when the first IRA bombs went off in central London, until the end of March 1976 there have been 297 bombs of one kind or another, 180 of them in London. Fifty-seven people have been killed, seventeen of them in London, as compared with 6,330 people killed by the motor vehicle in 1975 alone. Injuries from bombs in those three years, most of them slight, number 1,038, as compared with 317,000 road casualties in one year. Moreover, there have been one hundred arrests, thirty-six of them in London which are believed to account for about 70 per cent of all the incidents, an extraordinary rate of success in dealing with violent crime inspired by political or irrational motives. To put it in even more simple and perhaps more striking terms, we suffer in our whole country in one year less deaths by violence than the single City of Detroit suffered in 1974. Most of these murders are domestic or unpremeditated, or occur in circumstances in which the death penalty would certainly not apply. We nevertheless retain procedural rules of interrogation and trial originally intended to prevent the awful possibility of putting an innocent man to death. This demands an exceptionally high standard of proof of guilt and naturally makes the task of the prosecution difficult indeed. The real problem is, however, that you cannot have two systems of investigation and trial, one for the handful, say four or five, of capital murders and another for the nearly 2,000,000 other offences recorded each year, some of them regarded by public opinion as outrageous or disturbing. The practical effect is inevitably to lessen extensively the effectiveness of the criminal law as a deterrent to crime or as a means of catching and convicting criminals. Indeed, one of our most distinguished Judges, Lord Devlin, wrote in a recent book:

'If the success of a criminal prosecution is to be measured by the proportion of criminals whom it convicts and punishes, the English system must be regarded as a failure. Far too many people who have in fact committed crimes escape punishment. When a criminal goes free it is as much a failure of abstract justice as when an innocent man is convicted'.

I have no right to suggest that in your Canadian conditions judicial execution is not appropriate, but I am sure that in Britain it is too high a price to pay for the demonstrable ineffectiveness of the judicial system. I am, therefore, opposed to the death penalty, simply because its continuance prevents the reforms necessary to increase the effectiveness of criminal justice. The establishment of the truth rather than the determination of technical guilt ought in my view to be required of everyone involved in a criminal inquiry once irrevocable punishment is removed from the Statute Book. If, as our lawyers in Britain maintain, the objectives of justice are the protection of society, the deterrence of crime, the rehabilitation of the offender and the compensation of the victim, with punishment or retribution playing only a secondary part, it seems not unreasonable to suggest that the credibility of the suspected or accused person should be related, at least to some extent, to his spontaneity rather than to the results of the period of reflection and consultation between interrogation, arrest and trial. What we in Britain call the right of silence might have been designed by the criminals for their especial benefit and that of their professional advisers. It has done more to obscure the truth and facilitate crime than anything else in this century.

Its original justification was first quite properly that it afforded protection against self-incrimination in a process of justice in which punishment was the primary objective, and second that it afforded protection against police malpractice. The first justification in Great Britain is greatly diminished. The punishments of death and flogging have been abandoned. Though the zeal of the penal reformers is not matched by the willingness of successive governments to find the money to create and expand facilities for non-custodial treatment, it can at least be said that more and more people are coming to believe that criminal justice ought to have purposes more constructive and more humane than mere retribution or punishment.

The second justification has always been misconceived. The right of silence has always afforded the strongest motive for police malpractice. Conversely, its abolition will eliminate the strongest temptation for police misbehaviour. I do not, of course, imply that anyone should be compelled to speak. I mean that their willingness or unwillingness to answer questions should be a relevant consideration if they are tried for a criminal offence. To suggest this in Britain twenty years ago would have been regarded as heresy or worse. But since 1967 we have seen the abandonment after 600 years of the need for unanimity in jury verdicts. We now require also the pre-trial disclosure of alibi defences. Both these practices, incidentally, have been pursued in Scotland for many decades. One of the most distinguished legal committees ever set up in Britain, the Criminal Law Revision Committee consisting of judges and lawyers, both practising and academic, has recommended amongst other things, that the accused should be invited by the prosecution to enter the witness box, there to answer questions, or not, as he pleases. This suggestion has aroused bitter opposition from most practising lawyers, some of it sincere, some inspired by the desire to protect their own vested interests, but there is nothing more certain than that by the end of this century commonsense, logic and the public interest will prevail and the recommendation will be adopted, provided, of course, that there is no return to the death penalty.

The police are preparing the way for that reform by themselves demanding the introduction of a truly independent element in the system of examining and dealing with complaints from the public against our own members. We are the only public service to make such a demand, in sharp contrast to those who urge it upon us, but resist its application to themselves. I am confident that public reaction to the eventual scheme will raise the reputation of the police even higher than its present encouraging level, which has been revealed by three public opinion polls showing that the British police enjoy more public confidence than the church, the government, Parliament, the legal profession, the trade unions, the press and the armed forces. One of our most influential and unsentimental newspapers, the *Financial Times*, recently expressed a similarly encouraging assessment.

Not everything in our garden is, of course, lovely. Like you, like police forces everywhere, we have our problems, some of them acute. But the social and constitutional setting in which we work does at least allow us to view them objectively and to work for their solution.

I think most Western police forces today would say that their main problem is violent crime, homicides of all kinds and particularly homicides and violence in pursuance of theft. That is not the case in Britain. Crimes of violence do increase continually, but they amount to no more than 4 or 5 per cent of recorded crime and the rate of success in dealing with them is fairly high. I hope that does not sound complacent. Crimes of that kind will always be treated with the highest priority because of the sense of outrage and fear they provoke. But seen objectively they are a lesser cause for anxiety to police than the maintenance of our traditional high standards of good public order and tolerance and the protection of minorities at political demonstrations, trade disputes, football matches and in areas of social deprivation, heightened by our present economic difficulties with their consequent tensions and uneasiness. To maintain those standards we need more men, not just for the traditional preventive role, but to enable us to achieve a closer rapport with the people. Not only do we need more men, we need a better distribution of available manpower to the great cities where police problems are worst and conditions of service are least attractive.

We are already establishing a closer and more constructive relationship with the press than at any time in our history, not because we seek or expect any favours, but because we have nothing to hide and believe open administration to be the surest way to gain popular support.

Perhaps most important of all, we intend not merely to

protect tenaciously our freedom from political interference in operational matters but for the first time to exercise our right to tell the public direct through the communication media of our problems and our policies. For the last three years members of the London Metropolitan force have been authorised to speak freely to the press at station level about matters of fact within their knowledge, subject only to judicial rules and the right to privacy of individuals.

The National Police College at Bramshill in Hampshire offers the opportunity for men and women in all forces by qualifying examinations, extended interview and specialised impartial selection by boards including non-service personnel, to attend a variety of courses at junior, intermediate and senior command level and to read for a degree at any one of a number of universities, including Oxford and Cambridge, whilst still serving. About 115 men and women have graduated in this way and the prospects for achieving a high professional and academic standard for the service generally have never been so good.

I suppose you could sum up all that by saying that in Britain certainly, and I have no doubt elsewhere, the time has come when the police are abandoning their artisan status and are achieving by our ever-increasing variety of services, our integrity, our impartiality, our accountability and our dedication to the public good, a status not less admirable than that of the most learned and distinguished professions. The constable of 1829 or 1929 would have regarded that objective as a dream as unattainable as the climbing of Everest. For the constable of 1975 it is a clearly visible peak which he is rapidly climbing. We both have the honour in our respective areas to command proud and dedicated forces. I hope and believe that one day, like Tensing and Hillary, we may be shaking hands at the top.

But even assuming that in Britain and Canada we succeed in achieving standards of policing satisfactory to ourselves and to those we serve, it is they and they alone who must in the last resort determine the extent of our effectiveness. I will end by repeating the words I have used before.

It is high time that society stopped running away from the

problems of crime and wrongdoing and began to tackle them intelligently and courageously.

You must make up your minds what you really want. Absolute unrestricted freedom for the individual with all that this implies? Freedom to rob, freedom to steal? Freedom to break into shops and houses? Freedom to intimidate minorities by threats and violence? Do not think I am exaggerating when I say that this is part of the price you will pay increasingly for the continued enjoyment of liberty without responsibility. You can compensate the victim of criminal violence, you can provide free medical care for those who suffer it, you can encourage crime prevention and insurance to lessen the hardship arising from crime, but you will not reduce crime until you recognise that it is no longer enough for every citizen to play a negative part in law enforcement. The surest and quickest way to reduce crime and achieve a more humane and enlightened penal system is to increase the likelihood that the guilty will be convicted. If you are not willing to do this, you cannot hope to achieve any real progress in reducing crime or changing society's object in dealing with criminals. It is for you to decide.

4
A Compellable Witness*

Very few people understand that the extent to which the police forces of this country can succeed in their various tasks is governed by their limited resources and the criminal law itself. Most people are rather misled by television, the cinema, the crime novel; all giving the impression that the police are more numerous and more effective than they really are. The press, too, naturally give prominence to cases which the police have been able to bring to court and, understandably, rarely direct attention to the much greater number of cases which are never solved. About 70 per cent of all known crimes in London are never cleared up, but of course the proportion varies in different types of crime. For example, the success rate in dealing with homicide and serious assaults is very high, and will remain so. This is partly because the police will always give that kind of crime the highest priority and partly because half the crimes of violence not motivated by theft are committed by people whose identity is never in doubt. By contrast, success in dealing with burglary and theft will always be comparatively low. Such crimes are so numerous that the police cannot spend too much time on them. The chances of detection are low and, even if the identity of the wrongdoer is known, the procedures for investigation and trial are such as to restrict the likelihood of prosecution and conviction. If prosecution is

* Address to the Manchester Luncheon Club in April 1974; figures updated and with additions from an Address given in Caxton Hall, London, in February 1976. (This title implies the ability to require the accused to enter the witness box at the instance of the prosecution.)

possible, the consequent absorption of police resources during court proceedings can actually lessen the operational effectiveness of the force. The fifty-two-strong robbery squad in the Metropolitan Police, for example, which has so far enjoyed phenomenal success, is emasculated by the need for many of its members to kick their heels, sometimes for days, during lengthy court proceedings. Of course, no one wants a society in which there are too many policemen, in which police powers are excessive or in which the procedure of trial is unfair. The ideal is a reasonable balance between individual freedom and security for people and their property. We, therefore, have an interest in maintaining the fiction of a omniscient and effective police force because it is probably the best deterrent to crime, but in doing so we tend to conceal the difficulties and disadvantages which lessen our effectiveness.

The first and most important factor in determining the role, the numbers and the powers of the police is the naturally law-abiding nature of our community. This allows reliance on prevention rather than prosecution for the maintenance of an orderly society. Prosecution is not, as the fiction writer would have you believe, the primary activity of the police. It is in fact our last resort. Prevention depends, however, not just on social attitudes and propaganda but on a reasonable adequacy of police manpower. It is here that we come to one of our most serious and persistent problems, the long-lasting shortage of policemen where they are most needed – in Metropolitan London.

In 1921 there were 21,020 policemen in the Metropolitan force and 38,498 in the forces serving in the rest of England and Wales. By the end of 1975 the provincial forces had more than doubled their strength, while that of the Metropolitan force had increased by a mere 2 per cent. This has not been the result of conscious planning. It has resulted from a continuous increase in manpower in the forces outside London without any comparable effort to offset the strains and pressures of police duty in London by providing sufficiently effective inducements to serve in the metropolis.

No one could claim that this redistribution of manpower

over the last fifty years has been justified by a comparable change in operational needs. The two most disturbing features of the increase in crime, despite greater prosperity and better education, lie in the growth of crimes of violence motivated by theft and in juvenile crime. We had 56 robberies in 1921, about 4,500 last year; less than 4,000 burglaries in 1921, over 98,000 last year. The increase in workload is such that some years ago responsibility for offences triable summarily was allocated to the uniform branch in order to allow the CID to concentrate on more serious crime. Rather more than 50 per cent of crime falls within this category and, disregarding our mobile and specialist resources, we have only about three uniformed officers for each of our 787 square miles to deal with 269 burglaries and 359 thefts of and from cars reported daily. Entitlement to weekly and annual leave has greatly increased during those fifty years so that the actual availability of police manpower in London has dwindled more than the comparative figures show.

Of course, we have a variety of other tasks like traffic control and public order in its widest sense – hooliganism, vandalism, drugs, pornography and so on. Some problems are peculiar to London, notably four or five hundred political demonstrations yearly and the continual need to protect an increasing variety of persons and premises, particularly diplomatic missions. The promotion of harmony between the police and the immigrant community in London – as in some other parts of the country – has emerged as an important additional, sensitive and demanding task. It requires a lot of manpower, of training and above all of tolerance and self-control. The police bear the brunt of the immigrants' dissatisfaction with inequality of opportunity in jobs and housing. We suffer criticism, some of it unfair, and occasional provocation, with quite remarkable restraint and generally we maintain a fairness and balance which has contributed more than any other single factor to the avoidance of serious social disorder.

The concentration of police problems in London, coupled with the time and cost of travel, of housing, the need to work a longer week than other forces, the frequent cancellation of leave, sometimes at short notice, make the lot of the Metropolitan policeman much harder than that of his provincial colleagues. In 1973 the net loss of 513 officers included 238 who went to forces like Kent, Dorset, Hampshire, Thames Valley, Devon and Cornwall, where the grass presumably is greener. In 1975 the steady decrease in manpower was checked, partly by an increased London Allowance, partly by a lowering of the recruiting age, but mostly by increased general unemployment with its consequential anxieties about security in employment. In 1975 the Metropolitan force benefited from a net gain of 396 officers, of whom 156 were women, but despite a healthy improvement in recruitment during that year wastage continues to be a problem. In 1975 it amounted to 1,308, of whom 562 went on pension and 188 went to other forces. We seek continually to increase our strength, but in competition with industry, other forms of public service and of course other police forces we are not within sight of filling the shortfall of 5,200 men, or 20 per cent of our establishment. Fortunately the continual shortage of manpower has not been entirely harmful. It has compelled change and adaptation, notably a great increase in civilian staff, in the case of the Metropolitan force from just over 1,000 at the end of the Second World War to nearly 12,000 by the end of 1975; the shedding of duties not requiring police powers and training; and a transformation in mobility and communications. These changes are common in varying degrees to all forces, but are most striking in the Metropolitan, where a third of the present total manpower is civilian.

Even this seemingly beneficial change has disadvantages, seen at their worst in London, where the shortage of civil staff in the public services generally is acute and a high turnover lessens their usefulness. In the case of the most highly qualified and skilled civil support services, there can be special difficulties arising from relativities within the civil service. To take the fingerprint officers as an example: they must have five years' experience before qualifying as expert witnesses. They have been progressively – and most efficiently – taking over this work from the police over the last twenty years. Dissatisfaction with their pay is such that we lost 87 out of 288 in 1973. The remainder were at one time in that year working to rule, a sanction quite proper for them but denied by law to policemen. The result is that one of the most essential weapons in the police armoury is blunted and policemen themselves can do nothing about it. When you consider the vital importance of fingerprint evidence in some of the most important and difficult cases (the London bombers trial, for example) the dangers of this situation become painfully clear.

There has, of necessity, been a radical revision of the control over the use of such police manpower as we have. A policy committee, comprising the six senior police officers and three senior civilians, representing a total of 33,000 people, meets fortnightly to disclose information, discuss problems, suggest solutions, exercise delegated responsibility and initiate regular consultation with staff at operational and intermediate command level, the purpose being to ensure that the force acts as a corporate whole and not as a collection of seemingly unrelated and almost competitive departments. Our police manpower is mostly distributed between three principal departments, (a) prevention and public order, (b) traffic and (c) crime, but with proper coordination there are considerable benefits from overlapping. For example, all crimes triable in the magistrates' courts are assigned to the uniform branch. This is about half of all the crime. Two thirds of the CID, about 2,300 of 3,200 men, work under the direction of the uniform divisional commanders. This facilitates combined effort against troublesome epidemics which break out in different police divisions from time to time. Mugging, thefts from the person, malicious damage have all been effectively contained in this way. The more specialist CID at Scotland Yard have thus been able to concentrate on serious crime, on criminal intelligence and on 'target criminals', unhampered by theoretical responsibility for a great mass of what we call beat crime or minor crime.

No less important than this conservation and improved use of precious resources is the need to promote public confidence in the force. Our effectiveness depends greatly on the extent to which we can achieve the trust of the courts, the press and the public. This in turn depends on our willingness to be accountable and to deal effectively with our own wrong-doers. It is essential also that this willingness be made clear to the public. The unique degree of autonomy in investigating its own wrongdoing enjoyed by the CID from 1879 until 1972 did incalculable damage to its reputation and to its relationship with the detective branches of other forces, with the legal profession and with the courts generally. It is, of course, true that detectives in all police forces are subject to the temptations and pressures of corruption. Such tempta-tions, however, are much stronger in urban areas, particu-larly in London, because of the greater amount of serious crime and the large sums of money involved. The compara-tive immunity of the uniform branch from serious complaints does not indicate any fundamental difference in training or integrity. It simply reflects a growing and welcome parlia-mentary tendency during the last quarter of a century to remove by legislation the opportunities for corruption which had hitherto been common to police generally. Reform of the laws relating to betting and gaming, and a more enlightened public attitude to homosexuality and prostitution and other petty street offences lessened or eliminated the involvement of police in matters which had hitherto ensured an aura of distrust.

We have now made several important and related changes. The first governs the actual investigation of complaints against policemen. Until 1972, as already mentioned, the most serious complaints – those alleging crime – were investi-gated by the CID under the control of the Assistant Com-missioner (Crime). Only rarely was the help of other police forces invoked, although many of the more serious complaints were against the CID itself. This certainly did not satisfy the public, nor some complainants. To correct this we established A.10, a new branch of hand-picked CID and uniformed officers under the direct control of the Deputy Commissioner, operating day and night with supra-departmental authority. We also invoke the help of other forces in serious cases as a matter of routine and without hesitation. The effect on self-respect, on morale and on confidence between the uniform branch and the CID has been gratifying. No less encouraging is the increase in effectiveness in dealing with serious crime.

The second related change was to ask the Home Secretary to establish an Independent Review Authority to examine the way in which complaints against the police are investigated. The Metropolitan Police asked for this in 1972 and we must be unique in having led the demand for independent review of our own affairs. Not all of those who criticise us are willing to accept such measures in relation to their affairs.

Variations in the method of paying for overtime which had hitherto caused wide disparity between the take-home pay of CID and uniform officers opened the door to interchange between them, the intention being that every officer destined for intermediate or higher rank shall have served in both before reaching intermediate command. This began on 1 January 1976 and is probably the most significant and far-reaching order to have been issued within the Metropolitan force in this country.

The next step was to remove from the CID to the uniform branch the responsibility for dealing with obscene publications. It seems never to have been clearly understood that corruption from pornography in Soho has never related to fear of prosecution, because of the uncertainty of conviction and the derisory penalties imposed by the courts until comparatively recently. Corruption related rather to the need for protection against strong-arm gangs wishing to move into activities offering extremely high tax-free profits, a situation not unlike that of the violence inspired by prohibition in the United States. The police task was essentially preventive. Its assignment to the uniform branch allowed greater uniformity of enforcement, dispersal of responsibility, greatly increased supervision and thus greatly reduced temptation.

A further change was the radical revision of our relationship with the press. We had always adhered to the principle 'Tell them only what you must'. After consultation with most of the principal editors in London we reversed this to 'Withhold only what you must' and we delegated to station level the authority to disclose matters of fact not subject to judicial privacy or policies within the sphere of the Home Office. The force was told in writing that though the new policy might lead to occasional difficulties and embarrassment, no one acting in good faith would suffer, provided that he was frank and truthful. (The Memorandum dated May 1973 is printed as an appendix to this book.)

These changes can be summarised by saying 'we are putting our house in order, we have demanded that outsiders should be able to satisfy themselves that this is so and we have adopted, so far as we can, a policy of open administration'. It is too soon to assess the eventual effect of these policies but some of the present indications are very encouraging. We were warned that these changes would destroy the operational effectiveness of the force: not at all. Taken with a redistribution of resources within the CID and a much closer link-up of the CID with the chain of command in the force as a whole, they have produced much improved operational results. Armed bank robberies fell from sixty-five in 1972 to twenty-six in 1973; 150 alleged robbers were under arrest at the end of that year, very many more than at any time in this century. They were charged with some fifty-seven major robberies, going back as far as 1965 and involving a total of almost £3 million. Robberies as a whole were reduced in the year by 15 per cent, from 3,167 to 2,680. Muggings, which had more than doubled in four years to an average of 129 a month in 1972, fell in 1973 to 100 a month. The hi-jacking of lorries with high-value loads fell from 351 in 1973 to 98 in 1975. Although we cannot check the annual increase in crime generally, we can justifiably claim to have had outstanding and increasing success in dealing with really serious crime. In the last four years we have arrested more bank robbers than in any comparable period in our history. In fact, if we could secure a more rational distribution of manpower, available to the police of England and Wales as a whole, so that the strength was concentrated where it was most needed, we could achieve even more effective results.

So far as public confidence is concerned, we feel encouraged by three recent opinion polls which showed that there is now more confidence in the police than in any other public organisation or institution. About 30,000 men a year are deployed to deal with demonstrations and industrial disputes and their fortitude and good humour are a continual reminder of all that is best in English policing. In the ghettos – and let no one pretend that ghettos do not now exist – the courage, tolerance and sensitivity of the ordinary policeman is writing a new chapter in police history. It is not an overstatement to say that as a service we now demonstrate the Christian ethic in more practical terms than any section of our society, including the church.

Unfortunately there has emerged in the last few years an irreconcilable difference of opinion between the majority of the legal profession, which generally regards our system of investigation and trial as satisfactory, and the comparatively small number of experienced policemen who see it at close quarters, few if any of whom share that view. The issue is clouded by a lack of information and impartial research which alone will overcome prejudice on both sides.

It is wholly right that the press and public should express concern at the wrongful conviction of an innocent man. It is bad enough that a man should suffer injustice. It is even worse when public confidence in our system of justice is thereby undermined. But the scales of justice have two sides which ought to balance. The accuser is no less entitled to justice than the accused. A system of justice which denies that principle cannot enjoy confidence and respect and must provoke malpractice by those administering it. Of 94,042 persons arrested in New York City for felony in 1971, for example, only 552 went for trial, the result of plea-bargaining, reduced charges and the imbalance in civil rights. A sample of 136 arrests for the felonious possession of firearms similarly produced not one conviction for felony. Hardly surprising perhaps that crime should be a major preoccupation of American society or that American policemen should feel cynical disillusion, or resort to improper practices.

We are fortunately not in so unhappy a situation but it is essential that we do not drift towards it. Justice should be a matter of balance. Arguments for or against change should never be considered in isolation. They should always be viewed in the round. The seeming advantages of other systems should be set against their known disadvantages before they are recommended for adoption. Bail is a case in point. The present agitation is highly desirable and long overdue. But it is to be hoped that it will not exclude consideration of crimes committed by people on bail, of failure to surrender to bail, or the extent to which violence should lessen the likelihood of bail. Those who commend the experimental bail system in America usually make no mention of the known serious problem of crime by those on bail. And it might not be a bad idea to temper enthusiasm for reform with a little realism. The presumption of innocence, for example, was never meant to imply that every accused person is innocent. It means no more than that it is for the prosecution to discharge the burden of proof under rules affording protection to the accused against self-incrimination and possible punishment. Similarly, the verdict 'not guilty' does not mean that the accused is innocent or 'cleared' as the newspapers say. It is not the function of a court to determine innocence. Acquittals after remands in custody, when viewed against the system of justice as a whole, are in most cases more likely to be cause for congratulation than for tears.

If the police, the lawyers and the courts are doing their job properly the likeliest danger of wrongful conviction should and does arise from mistaken identity. I believe that many policemen are sympathetic to the demand for a higher standard of proof when identification is the most important issue and will welcome the reforms now under discussion.

The argument that to abolish the caution and to allow the prosecution to invite the accused to enter the witness box would increase the powers of the police in some mysterious way should at least be countered by the argument that such changes would lessen appreciably any rational motive for police misbehaviour and could have the gradual effect of transferring part of the interrogation process from the police station to the court, where everyone could hear it. The widely held belief of lawyers that justice on the whole works well should be examined against the no less widely held view of policemen that in some important areas it does not; and that the police more than anyone else bear the brunt of that failure. The radical image of an omniscient police force with sweeping powers should be contrasted with the actuality of a comparatively small, undermanned and overworked force doing its best to contain its problems in the face of continual criticism and harassment. The adversary system itself requires of policemen willingness to suffer continual attack day after day, some of it fair, much of it unfair, a great deal of it damaging to our reputation and to our morale, and with no redress. The best protection for the police from unfair criticism, from misunderstanding of their role or from the disadvantages of the legal system is a willingness to expose and discuss their problems and to allow the public as free access as can lawfully be possible.

We cannot in the meantime turn away from our problems, of which the most pressing now are violent crime motivated by theft, terrorism (by which I mean bombing, hi-jacking, threats of kidnapping or killing and so on) and the need to gain the respect and confidence of the immigrant community and, perhaps the most tiresome, the instant wiseacres on radio and television without whom no newsworthy incident is nowadays complete. In the midst of all the turbulence and argument natural to a free society the police must continue to take the strain with fortitude, with moderation and with tolerance. We need all those virtues today more than ever before; and there is, in my view, no sign that they are not amply forthcoming.

5
Minority Verdict[*]

Introduction

People are very interested in sin and crime and this curiosity
is continually satisfied by the journalist, the crime novelist,
the film and television producer. Now most of them are
understandably more concerned to entertain rather than to
enlighten, but it is largely from them that you get your ideas
about the police. You are reminded of us daily by the newspapers, television and radio, so much so that we are accepted
as a part of daily life, rather like the weather.

But most people rarely have anything to do with the police.
Most of you don't break the law, at least not in ways likely to
attract our attention. Even in London the chances of first-
hand contact are not high. Of London's 8 million citizens we
last year arrested about 148,000, counting everyone, teen-
agers, children who were never prosecuted, offenders of
all kinds from serious criminals to drunks. That's only about
seven or eight arrests in the year for every member of the
force, a figure that might be surprising to some of you. Those
who come to us as victims, their homes burgled or their cars
stolen, are also comparatively few. The result is that most of
you have impressions of the police vaguely fashioned by
crime stories, by Dixon or Barlow, and the chances are that
these impressions will be pretty far from the truth.

There can be no doubt about the importance of the police.
In theory your safety and your liberty depend upon the laws

* The Dimbleby Lecture, BBC television, November 1973.

and the constitution, but in practice the decisions of Parliament and the courts would count for very little if the police were not there to enforce them.

Police Powers

Some people think that this makes us a powerful body. Power is an emotive word, particularly in relation to the police. It suggests a right to punish at will, free from effective control. In fact, of course, we have no such power. Our development has always been conditioned by two conflicting needs: one to maintain order and protect people, the other to ensure that we ourselves do not act unreasonably or oppressively. For this reason the police have always remained few in number and answerable to the general law. We have no special immunities. A policeman who breaks the law is prosecuted and punished just like anyone else. The only power we possess is the power to inconvenience by bringing people before the courts, and even then we are at risk if we use that power improperly, or unfairly. The fact that the British police are answerable to the law, that we act on behalf of the community and not under the mantle of government, makes us the least powerful, the most accountable and therefore the most acceptable police in the world.

It is truer to say that a policeman discharges responsibilities than that he exercises powers. He is only an ordinary member of the community who has undertaken certain duties on behalf of his fellow citizens. These responsibilities have grown wider and more complicated. When most people were humble, ignorant and poor, it was comparatively easy to do our job without effective criticism. Authority as such was respected. But society today is better equipped to question political motives and decisions and dissent is now a vehicle of social change. But, of course, this new freedom is bound to create strains within the community.

The problem is aggravated by other factors. We are an insular and conservative people, asked in one generation to become a tolerant multi-racial society, Inequality of opportunity in jobs and housing does not make the change any

easier. So the maintenance of order, particularly in the great
cities, is now one of our most important duties. It differs
significantly from maintaining order in an earlier age.
Dissent nowadays originates not so much from the slums as
from highly educated radicals and organised labour. It enjoys
wide public support and is viewed by the courts at all levels
with a tolerance that would have astonished their fore-
bears.

The brief imprisonment of five London dockers in 1973 is
a far cry from the Tolpuddle martyrs. This does not mean
that there is support for the extremist. The terrorist or the
urban guerilla, though eminently newsworthy, is a nuisance
rather than a threat to society. He may injure or kill; he may
destroy property; but his activities are certain to alienate the
community from his cause.

Four Stages of Justice

Of all the problems with which the police have to contend,
undoubtedly the most continuous is the prevention and
investigation of crime. But you must remember that this is
only one part of our system of criminal justice. You should
think of it as having four successive stages. First comes the
enactment by Parliament of the criminal laws, secondly the
task of the police to enforce them. The third stage is the
criminal trial, where the question of guilt is decided. Finally,
there is the problem of what to do with the guilty. Each of
these four stages has usually been considered in isolation.
Each tends to be the province of a different group of people.
Politicians make the laws, police enforce them, lawyers run
the trials, and the prison or probation services deal with
convicted offenders. None of these groups is obliged to give
much thought to the problems of the others or to consider the
working of the system as a whole.

Now this is unfortunate because the different parts of the
system are intimately connected. It is no good Parliament
passing laws if the people cannot enforce them. There is no
point in catching criminals if the system of trial is so in-

efficient that it lets them go free. Savage punishments serve no purpose if very few offenders are actually caught and punished. Equally, Parliament and the police are wasting their time if penalties are so small that it pays people to go on offending. Put like that you may think these points self-evident, but in practice people often fail to make the necessary connection. That is why I'm going to have quite a lot to say (and I ought to make it clear that I am saying it on my own responsibility) about aspects of justice which you may think are strictly not the business of the police – the criminal law, the system of trial and the question of punishment.

Take, for example, the criminal law. Our attempts to enforce some laws are bound to be regarded by some people without enthusiasm or even with downright hostility. In fact, the only crimes we can tackle knowing that we shall have your full support are those which provoke a sense of public outrage. Murder in the course of theft or rape, violence against women, children or old people, robbery, are obvious examples. But these are few in number: only about 3 or 4 per cent of crime. By contrast, trying to enforce controversial laws, like those about illegal immigration or trade disputes, provokes reactions ranging from pained criticism to physical resistance. Those who oppose new laws don't abandon their opposition when the laws reach the Statute Book, they redirect it against the police. However illogical or unfair, we must accept this as a fact of life. People often feel so strongly about the issues which provoke demonstrations or strikes that they find it difficult to see why they should not give forcible expression to their views. But the use of force in these situations is a serious threat to our democracy. We cannot allow some people to use or condone violence which denies freedom to others. Free speech and the right to work are among the rights guaranteed by the law and it is the duty of the police to uphold them. We often find this task extremely difficult. It calls for tact, firmness, tolerance and self-control to an extent not always appreciated. You may remember that in the summer of last year we had some lively demonstrations by London dockers. As a result, we were accused by the right wing of being weak, vacillating and indecisive, and by the left of being unreasonable, arbitrary and brutal. Perhaps that means we got it about right. At any rate, there were no significant casualties, except perhaps the truth.

It is almost as difficult to deal with offences which people, for one reason or another, don't feel strongly about or don't think of as morally wrong. Motoring offences are the best example, but the same thing can be said of crimes like evading tax or fiddling expenses which are difficult to detect, so that those who are caught look as if they have been unfairly singled out for punishment. We tend to be criticised both for enforcing laws and for failing to enforce them. People sometimes expect results which the state of the law and public opinion simply will not allow.

Police and Pornography

A good example of this is the recent campaign about pornography. The Metropolitan Police were accused, unsuccessfully, of failing to exercise their powers to enforce the laws against pornography. It was said that we could clean up Soho in a few days if only we were willing to do so and, despite the pressure of business in the High Court and the Court of Appeal, priority was given to deciding the issues involved. The truth is that pornography is very difficult to control. The point at which it becomes unlawful is almost impossible to define, so that contested prosecutions are rather like a game of chance. There is no power of arrest and cases take a long time to come on, at present several months in the lower Court, and a year in the higher. Hard core pornography remains available at particular premises despite police action. One address in Soho was raided no less than thirty-five times in twelve months, the occupant no doubt having decided that the profits far outweighed the risks. Prosecutions can be lengthy and expensive, and even if successful the penalties are usually no more than a light tax on an extremely profitable trade.

Do not think that I am criticising the lightness of these fines. They are mostly determined by the maximum penalties open to the courts. We are short of men and – even if we were not – we must have some scale of priorities. If the rate of convictions and the penalties are any indication of how seriously the community regards obscene publications, it is hardly sensible to expect us to put hundreds of men on to cleaning up Soho. They would only increase the backlog of cases awaiting trial. There have even been suggestions that pornographers buy immunity by corrupting the police. This would be a most unbusinesslike thing to do. It's far cheaper to pay the fines than to incur the expense and risk of trying to bribe a policeman.

Our experience with pornography shows that some activities, even if most people think them undesirable or offensive, cannot, in practice, be stopped. The most one can hope for is to regulate the way in which they are carried on. Gambling, brothel-keeping, unconventional sexual practices are all in this category. There is no certainty that very severe penalties would suppress them. The demand will always be there. A more likely effect is that they would be driven underground, raising the cost to the consumer and the profit to those willing to take the risks. The incentive to oppose or corrupt the police would be greatly increased. Prohibition in the United States, which created a climate in which gangsters could thrive, is surely the classic example of a self-defeating attempt to eradicate the ineradicable.

What is needed is to find the right balance, to achieve a degree of control acceptable to the public and, at the same time, enforceable in practice. Those who frame new laws sometimes give insufficient weight to the difficulties of enforcement. They devote much time and care to debating the moral implications but assume, often quite wrongly, that people can be made to obey them. Once enacted, some laws are dumped like unwanted babies on the back door of the police station with little or no inquiry as to their eventual health. Some of them are found to be stillborn and others are dying for lack of teeth. Public criticism of their ineffectiveness is usually directed to the police rather than to difficulties over which the police have no control, such as the process of trial.

Trial by Jury

What about our system of trial? In particular, the trial by jury of serious offenders. I suppose that most of you believe that our system of trial is the best in the world. If it doesn't quite attain perfection, it's only because of the fallible human beings who celebrate the sacred rites in the temple of justice. I used these rather heavy religious metaphors because the public's confidence in our present system of trial by jury is essentially a matter of faith. It is based on practically no evidence whatever. No one has ever thought it necessary to make a full, practical and impartial investigation of how the system works. Indeed, in the present state of the law no such investigation is possible.

Take, for example, the jury, the very heart of the criminal trial. There is very little reliable information about how and why juries arrive at their verdicts because no one is allowed to listen to the discussions in the jury room. Lawyers obviously believe that public confidence in the jury would be undermined if this were allowed to happen. I find this curious. If exposing the truth about the jury would destroy the public's belief in its value, then surely it is high time that belief was destroyed. I cannot think of any other social institution which is protected from rational inquiry because investigation might show that it was not doing its job.

Let me make it clear that I am not making an attack on trial by jury. What I am complaining about is the atmosphere of sacred mystery which always obscures any discussion of the jury. Of course, I have my private views about juries, based on my own experience. For example, I think that it is very important to retain juries in offences against the state, like trials under the Official Secrets Act. On the other hand, I find it difficult to imagine a more inefficient way of trying a complicated fraud case. But these are my views and I do not claim that they are any more scientific than those of other people, who may think differently. The fact is that no one has the evidence upon which it would be possible to make a fair assessment. What I would like to see is a careful and detailed study to provide us with the material upon which we could evaluate trial by jury. And although I know that it would be a big undertaking, I would like to see the study cover the whole system of criminal justice.

What we do know about trials in higher courts doesn't justify any complacency. Indeed, there is one fact I can mention which should be enough in itself to demand some kind of inquiry. This is the rate of acquittals. Of all the people in England and Wales who plead not guilty and are tried by jury, about half are acquitted. You may perhaps say to yourselves, 'Well why not? Perhaps they really were innocent. How do the police know that they were guilty?' But things are not quite so simple. For one thing, the English criminal trial never decides whether the accused is innocent. The only question is whether, in accordance with the rules of evidence, the prosecution has proved that he is guilty – and this is not at all the same thing. There may be all kinds of reasons why the jury do not think that the prosecution has proved guilt. They may think that he probably did it but that the defence has raised some reasonable doubt. Or sometimes a piece of evidence which would have put the matter beyond doubt is not available, or is excluded by the rules of evidence. Occasionally they are just taken in by a false, but plausible story, or by an exceptionally persuasive advocate. You must not, therefore, think anyone who is acquitted must have been innocent. There are many other possible explanations. But one thing is certain. Every acquittal is a case in which either a guilty man has been allowed to go free or an innocent citizen has been put to the trouble and expense of defending himself.

The 'Failure Rate'

There must be some rate of failure. We cannot always expect to convict the guilty or never to prosecute the innocent. But in my opinion a failure rate of one in two is far too high. I doubt whether it would be tolerated in many other kinds of activity, so I think it is something that certainly needs looking into. In the absence of any reliable research no one can say with any certainty why the acquittal rate is so high. A fairly high number of acquittals are undoubtedly by direction of the judges, as soon as they have heard the prosecution case. Since 1967 cases are no longer sifted effectively by a magistrate, and the higher courts are cluttered up by cases which in my opinion should never have got there at all. This probably accounts for what seems to be an increase since 1966 from 39 per cent to about 50 per cent in acquittals and tends to obscure the problem I am discussing.

My own view is, nevertheless, that the proportion of those acquittals relating to those whom experienced police officers believe to be guilty is too high to be acceptable. That opinion is admittedly not universal. Many people, particularly lawyers, would disagree. When Lord Elwyn Jones, the former Attorney General, was once asked why the acquittal rate in some Welsh counties was as high as 90 per cent, he said, 'Well, ladies and gentlemen, Welsh juries are generally in favour of justice, but they're not bigoted about it'. I wouldn't deny that sometimes commonsense and humanity produce an acquittal which could not be justified in law, but this kind of case is much rarer than you might suppose. Much more frequent are the cases in which the defects and uncertainties in the system are ruthlessly exploited by the knowledgeable criminal and by his advisers.

The object of a trial is to decide whether the prosecution has proved guilt. It is, of course, right that in a serious criminal case the burden of proof should be upon the prosecution. But in trying to discharge that burden the prosecution has to act within a complicated framework of rules which were designed to give every advantage to the defence. The prosecution has to give the defence advance notice of the whole of its case, but the accused, unless he wants to raise an alibi, can keep his a secret until the actual trial. When the police interrogate a suspect or charge him they have to keep reminding him that he need not say anything. If he has a criminal record the jury are not ordinarily allowed to know about it. Most of these rules are very old. They date from a time when, incredible as it may seem, an accused person was not allowed to give evidence in his own defence, when most accused were ignorant and illiterate. There was no legal aid and, perhaps most important, if someone was convicted he would most likely be hanged or transported. Under these conditions it is not surprising that the judges who made the rules were concerned to give the accused every possible protection. But it is, to say the least, arguable that the same rules are not suited to the trial of an experienced criminal, using skilled legal assistance, in the late twentieth century.

The Trial as a Contest

The criminal and his lawyers take every advantage of these technical rules. Every effort is made to find some procedural mistake which will allow the wrongdoer to slip through the net. If the prosecution evidence is strong the defence frequently resorts to attacks on prosecution witnesses, particularly if they are policemen. They will be accused as a matter of routine of perjury, planting evidence, intimidation or violence. What other defence is there, when found in possession of drugs, explosives or firearms, than to say they were planted? Lies of this kind are a normal form of defence, but they are sure to be given extensive publicity. In many criminal trials the deciding factor is not the actual evidence but the contest between a skilled advocate and a policeman or other witness under this kind of attack, often part of what Lord Devlin calls 'The world of fantasy created by a defence counsel at a loss for anything better to do on behalf of his client'.

The advocates for the defence are, for the most part, only doing their job. They are there to get their client off. In a hopeless or unpopular case this can be a distasteful task. To be a criminal lawyer needs professional knowledge, integrity and, when acting for the defence, moral courage. Whatever his personal feelings about the case the lawyer must devote himself to the cause of his client with all the persuasion and skill at his command. At the same time he also owes a duty to the cause of justice and the ethics of his profession. He must not put forward a defence which he knows to be false. It is not for a defence lawyer to judge his client's case. However unlikely his story may sound he is entitled to have it heard. But it is a different matter for an advocate to say things which he knows to be deliberate lies. To do this is not to take part in the administration of justice but to help to defeat it. Most lawyers observe very high standards. They manage to serve both their clients' and the public interest honourably and well; so much so that most of them tend to be frankly incredulous when it is suggested that there are some other lawyers who do not. The kind of behaviour I have in mind is often easy for the police to recognise but almost impossible to prove.

I cannot obviously discuss identifiable cases, but I can describe the practices I mean.

We see the same lawyers producing, off the peg, the same kind of defence for different clients. Prosecution witnesses suddenly and inexplicably change their minds. Defences are concocted far beyond the intellectual capacity of the accused. False alibis are put forward. Extraneous issues damaging to police credibility are introduced. All these are part of the stock-in-trade of a small minority of criminal lawyers. The truth is that some trials of deliberate crimes for profit – robbery, burglary and so on – involve a sordid, bitter struggle of wits and tactics between the detective and the lawyer. Public accusations of misconduct, however, have always been one-sided, with the result that doubts about the criminal trial mostly centre upon police conduct, as if the police alone had a motive for improper behaviour. Let there be no doubt that a minority of criminal lawyers do very well from the proceeds of crime. A reputation for success, achieved by persistent lack of scruple in the defence of the most disreputable, soon attracts other clients who see little hope of acquittal in any other way. Experienced and respected metropolitan detectives can identify lawyers in criminal practice who are more harmful to society than the clients they represent.

A conviction said to result from perjury or wrongdoing by police rightly causes a public outcry. Acquittal, no matter how blatantly perverse, never does, even if brought about by highly paid forensic trickery. Of course I speak in general terms. I would like to be more specific but for obvious reasons I cannot. I am conscious too that people who make general accusations can be said to be willing to wound and yet afraid to strike. This does not mean that such general accusations ought not sometimes to be made. They are often made against the police, no doubt for similar reasons; nor are they always without substance.

I ought perhaps to give you two examples to illustrate what I mean. The first is a form of questioning to smear a member of the Flying Squad of unblemished character giving evidence in a strong case. 'Are you a member of the Flying Squad? And is it not a fact that four or more members of that Squad are presently suspended on suspicion of corruption?' Before the judge can intervene the damage is done. The jury is influenced by the smear in direct contravention of the principles governing the criminal trial. That kind of theme is played extensively and with infinite variations.

The second example is what Conan Doyle would have called 'the Curious Case of the Bingo Register'. This was a case in which a hardened criminal burgled a flat and wounded one of the elderly occupants very badly. He was identified, arrested, denied the offences and was remanded to prison. A month after committal for trial his solicitor disclosed an alibi defence which suggested that he was playing bingo at a club on the night of the offence and had signed the visitors' book. Inquiry showed that the prisoner had actually signed the book at the foot of the relevant page but that unfortunately for him the two preceding and the two following signatures were those of people with different surnames who had visited the club in one group and signed the book together. The signature could, therefore, only have been entered later and, it would seem, must have been written in prison. The prosecution notified the defence of their findings. Defence counsel thereupon withdrew from the case, as indeed did the instructing solicitor. The prisoner, on the advice of his new solicitor and counsel, pleaded 'guilty' and the matter rested there. It was not, of course, possible to prove who had taken the visitors' book to prison, although the prison authorities pointed out drily that only a visit by a lawyer or his clerk would be unsupervised and such visits had occurred. This was, in fact, a painstaking attempt to establish a false alibi for a dangerous persistent criminal. The police looked upon the case as remarkable only in that they were able to prove the falsity of the alibi.

The Policeman's Sense of Commitment

Because of its technicality and its uncertainty, the criminal trial has come to be regarded as a game of skill and chance in which the rules are binding on one side only. It is hardly surprising that a policeman's belief in its fairness should decline as he gathers experience, or that he should be tempted to depart from the rules. The detective is the person most affected because it is he who regularly bears the brunt of the trial process. In theory he is devoted only to the cause of justice. He likes to think of himself as having no personal interest in acquittal, conviction or sentence and that his career is not affected by the outcome of his cases. In practice this is a gross oversimplification. Most detectives have a strong sense of commitment. It would be unnatural if they did not feel personally involved in some of their cases and it would be untrue to suggest that they are not sometimes outraged by the results. All are under occasional temptation to bend the rules to convict those whom they believe to be guilty, if only because convention has always inhibited them from saying how badly they think those rules work. A few may sometimes be tempted also to exploit the system for personal gain. A detective who finds general acceptance of a system which protects the wrongdoer can come to think that if crime seems to pay for everyone else, why not for him? The next step may be to demand money for not opposing bail, for not preferring charges, for omitting serious charges, for a share in the stolen property and so on. Not many, even of those who regard the system with cynical disillusion, give way to that kind of temptation, but it is no help to pretend that it does not happen. As a policeman I believe in the virtue of confession for ourselves no less than for our customers. In the past we have paid heavily and unnecessarily in loss of public confidence by trying to conceal or minimise the wrongdoing of a very few. I think it absolutely essential to expose it and to deal with it ruthlessly. Even a little corruption of that kind does untold damage to the reputation of a service which little deserves it.

Complaints Against the Police

Some of you may have heard of the new A.10 Branch that we in the Metropolitan Police have created to deal with complaints against policemen. I think that most people who have had any dealings with A.10 will agree that it has demonstrated beyond any doubt our willingness and ability to deal swiftly and effectively with our own wrongdoers. Well over 100 officers have left the force, voluntarily or otherwise, since the change of system for investigating complaints. We realise, however, the procedure has one major drawback. It looks like a judgement of policemen by other policemen. So long as this remains the case some of you will perhaps be, understandably, sceptical. No one likes to accept the verdict of a person thought to be a judge in his own cause. That is why the Home Office are trying to devise a system of outside review of such investigations which will have everyone's confidence. It is not easy, but the sooner that this obstacle to public confidence can be overcome the better, for the police more than anyone else. I think an independent review will do much to dispel such distrust as remains. False accusations against the police in court are all the more effective when juries know that similar accusations have sometimes been shown to be true. It is sad but understandable that opposition to some of the recent proposals for reforming the system of trial has been based less on evidence or logic than upon distrust of the police.

But when you consider the arguments put forward in defence of the present rules of trial, it is important for you to appreciate that there may be vested interests in their continuance. The practice of criminal law, either as solicitor or barrister, is not a public service. It is done for money. The more subtle the rules and doubtful the outcome, the more opportunity for the advocate to show his skill on either side. On the other hand, if the criminal trial were less of a game, lawyers would not be able to have so much effect on the verdict. I can't help thinking that that would be a good thing. It is wrong that a man should need an expensive lawyer to establish his innocence. Nor should skilful lawyers be able to secure the acquittal of the guilty.

Consider the implications of the famous BBC 'Face to Face' interview between Mr John Freeman and the late Lord Birkett, whom he described as one of the three or four greatest criminal lawyers of this century:

Freeman: Do you happen to remember how many successful murder defences you undertook in your career at the Bar?

Birkett: If it doesn't sound immodest, it's easier to remember those in which I failed.

Freeman: Well how many did you fail in?

Birkett: Well, three I think.

Freeman: Out of many dozens?

Birkett: Out of many dozens, yes.

Freeman: Now I want to ask you, did you yourself always believe in the innocence of your clients when you defended them?

Birkett: To be quite frank, no.

Freeman: Would you think it was your duty as counsel to use every possible trick within the law to get a man acquitted?

Birkett: Well I don't like the word 'trick'. I would be against tricks of all kinds. But I think if you would alter the question to saying, 'Do you regard it as your duty to do everything within your power within the rules, to get him acquitted?', I would say yes.

Freeman: Have you ever got a man acquitted or a woman acquitted, on a murder charge, whom you believe in your heart to be guilty?

Birkett: Yes.

Freeman: Any regrets about that?

Birkett: No.

Those of you who are unfamiliar with the process of criminal justice may now find it rather easier to understand

Dr Johnson's comment that a lawyer has no business with the justice or injustice of the cause which he undertakes. You may also find it easier to understand that when lawyers and policemen speak of justice they are not necessarily speaking of the same thing. The lawyer is often speaking of fair play according to the rules. The policeman is speaking of the establishment of the truth with which the system of criminal justice is not necessarily concerned. This at least can be said, that those police officers who are closely concerned with our present system of investigation and trial do not share the complacency with which it is viewed by lawyers generally.

Are Penalties Adequate?

Many people think that the answer to crime is to punish more severely but I doubt whether this is often true. Failure to deal with deliberate crime does not have much to do with the penalties being inadequate. The real causes lie in the inefficiency of the earlier stages of the process: the stages of investigation and trial. I do not think that professional criminals carry on their trade because they take a light view of the punishments which the law may inflict. It is rather because they think that they have an excellent chance of escaping punishment altogether. There is a fair amount of evidence to encourage them in this belief. Some of the most notorious post-war criminals have had the better of many encounters with the law, chalking up several acquittals before the final downfall. Of course I am not saying that punishments do not matter. There is no point in convicting people if you then pat them on the back and let them go. But I do think that our present scale of punishments would, in most cases, be perfectly adequate if only we could improve the rates of detection and of conviction.

Demands for heavier punishments seem to me to reflect frustration at our apparent inability to check the growth of crime, particularly those crimes involving violence. But they always stop short at emotional appeal and blind belief. Few people seem aware, for example, that a high proportion of crimes of violence are cleared up, because the identity of many of the wrongdoers is known at the outset and because the police, understandably, give a high priority to the remainder. The overall picture of crime is not at all what you might suppose from newspapers and television. The most troublesome aspect has been the increase in crimes of violence motivated by theft, which now shows signs of diminishing or at least levelling out, and the extent to which young people indulge in violence often without rational motive. But the remainder of the picture ought not to be distorted by emotion. It has in fact a number of encouraging features.

There is no crisis in law and order, whatever people may say. We are still a generally law-abiding nation. Our criminal law now values life more highly than property. Since the war it has been adapted to current attitudes and standards to a quite remarkable extent. Betting, gaming, prostitution, homosexuality, abortion, present few serious problems to the police as compared with the aura of corruption, distrust and resentment generated by some of those activities in the thirties. We continue to look on the private possession of firearms as vaguely anti-social and their use by criminals as outrageous. The police themselves object to being armed, other than for exceptional and dangerous tasks. We are free from political interference in operational matters. Our non-elective judges are similarly free from political interference and rightly enjoy a worldwide reputation for integrity and impartiality. The effect of crime on the individual who experiences it, though unpleasant, has never been more widely offset, either by private insurance or the welfare state. The Criminal Injuries Compensation Board last year paid more than £3 million to the criminally assaulted. There is nothing in our present situation to justify hasty or extreme change, notwithstanding the emotion aroused by reports of particular crimes like mugging and bombing. That some change is necessary is, I think, beyond doubt, but it should reflect consideration of the system as a whole, and it should aim at increased effectiveness rather than more severe punishment.

The more effective the law in establishing the truth, or, if you like, responsibility, the less people will want to hit out with drastic penalties. There are, I think, two needs: the first, obvious and not controversial, an increase in police manpower, in London in particular; the second, highly controversial, a change in both investigation and trial to make the discovery of the truth more likely. That might be achieved by relating the credibility of the accused person at least to some extent to his spontaneity rather than to that period of reflection and consultation between arrest and trial which, as I have mentioned earlier, has produced some of the most ingenious, predictable, and profitable fiction of our time. But that, of course, is a suggestion which would require a lecture on its own.

Unwillingness to make the law more effective will inevitably provoke demands for harsher punishments and will increase the pressures on the police to use more arbitrary methods. You can already see this in the United States where a society of great wealth and outstanding achievement is marred by a system of justice notorious for ineffectuality, corruption and violence. A land of opportunity indeed – not least for the criminal, the lawyer and the gunsmith. If we in Great Britain are to continue to police by consent, rather than by the para-military system they have in the United States and many other countries, we must avoid a drift to alienation of police and people. Our system of justice must be respected by the people for being effective without being unjust, and maintained by a police force that is efficient without being repressive.

Some people cling to a curious, old-fashioned belief that there is something vaguely improper in a policeman talking about the law, the courts and lawyers. No doubt the General Staff felt the same way about the infantryman on the Somme. But as Lord Devlin said, 'The police have a right to demand that the path they must tread should be clearly designed to lead to a just result for the community for whom they act, as well as for the accused'. You simply cannot ask men to do one of the more difficult and sometimes dangerous jobs of our time and expect them not to reason why. Or if you do, you will be unlikely to get the kind of men you want. The policeman knows as much about crime and investigation as anyone. Of course his view should not necessarily prevail.

But it should be heard. It may be the verdict of a minority, but our system of justice is too important to be left to any one section of society, lawyers or police. It should be the concern of all.

6

Social Violence*

A degree of controlled violence is essential to government as we understand it. Certainly that is true for the armed forces and the police. Both may be required to use violence for a variety of purposes: to defend the homeland from external attack, to uphold basic freedoms such as the right to own property, to express political views and so on. Any form of government known to us relies upon the ultimate sanction of violence as the only certain means of preventing anarchy and most of us accept this without worrying too much about the varying circumstances in which it is used, possibly because of a conscious or unconscious awareness of the accountability of the users to Parliament, the courts or, in the last resort, to public opinion.

Reaction to violence not only affects the attitudes adopted by one country to another (the persecution of minorities, for example) but different sections of the same community towards each other (the rugby/cricket anti-apartheid demos). I think we have to find an agreed point from which to begin a discussion on so confusing and complex a subject. Perhaps this comment by General Sir John Hackett, Principal of King's College, London, will do:

'There is no sign whatever that man will soon desist from the application of physical force to the solution of social problems. Force still remains the ultimate sanction in human

* Address to the Royal College of Defence Studies in August 1971; figures updated.

affairs and this is likely so be so as far as we can see. Armed
forces are therefore of high importance to sovereign states for
without them sovereignty can only be exercised in diminishing degree.'

I imagine that comment is acceptable to most people. It
sounds reasonable and simple to understand, particularly so
in relation to our own countries. For some of you it might
even have a certain nostalgia, like the yearning of a New
York leader writer for the good old days when air was clean
and sex was dirty. But how about the following mildly
satirical comment by Roger Woddis in the *New Statesman*?

Ethics for Everyman

Throwing a bomb is bad,
Dropping a bomb is good;
Terror, no need to add,
Depends on who's wearing the hood.

Kangaroo courts are wrong,
Specialist courts are right;
Discipline by the strong,
Is fair if your collar is white.

Company output 'soars',
Wages, of course, 'explode';
Profits deserve applause,
Pay-claims, the criminal code.

Daily the Church declares
Betting-shops are a curse;
Gambling with stocks and shares
Enlarges the national purse.

Workers are absentees,
Businessmen relax,
Different as chalk and cheese;
Social morality
Has a duality –
One for each side of the tracks.

Does not that suggest to you that reaction to social violence is
likely to be affected by the extent to which the society in
which it occurs is generally regarded as equitable and just?
Whether it is, in fact, equitable and just is a matter of opinion
which will vary as political awareness matures, and as

literacy, education and communication improve. We in this island have long regarded ourselves as an example for the world of government by consent, of individual freedom and of political and religious tolerance. It is an image which has only been retained by a willingness to give way to changes which have not always been painless or non-violent and of which acceptance has often been grudging.

Not all social violence is related perceptibly to conditions offering scope for the apologist; to political or religious issues, conditions of employment, academic freedom and so on. Most of it arises from ordinary human characteristics; selfishness, greed, ambition, lust and so on, leading to violence against persons and against property, ranging from murder and assaults to burglary and malicious damage. Some has no rational motive that we can discern; the hooliganism of football and holiday crowds, for example. I think for our discussion it will be convenient to accept a distinction between violence which most societies regard as ordinarily criminal, such as murder, robbery, burglary, assaults and hooliganism; and violence which can loosely be said to arise from dissatisfaction with social conditions; political demonstrations, trade disputes, university sit-ins and so on.

Violence arising from crime is regarded with disapproval by all classes of society. Whatever problems it poses for particular communities, it is never likely to threaten their stability or security, unless related in the minds of a significant minority to a popular cause in the second category I mentioned, that of social justice (e.g. the Irish struggle for Home Rule, the Jewish struggle in Palestine, the racial struggle in America). But in many sophisticated societies, violence arising from crime is regarded as one of the more serious current problems so perhaps we should consider it first.

It is always assumed that crimes of violence have increased and are increasing, both in this country and in other similar societies. The statistics certainly allow such an assumption. In England and Wales, for example, known crimes of violence against the person (murder, manslaughter, infanticide, woundings and assaults) have risen from 4,800 in 1949 to 13,100 in 1959, to 36,600 in 1969 and to 62,800 in 1974; during the same period violent offences against property have risen from 92,000 to 493,000. Robbery alone has increased from 990 to 8,670 cases.

An average of 100,000 crimes per annum was recorded between 1900 and 1919; in 1939 it rose to 300,000 and in 1947 almost 500,000. In 1974 the number was roughly 2 million.

Loss of life from crime is nevertheless very small indeed in relation to the size of the population; similarly, serious physical injury is comparatively rare. That violent crime is increasing is beyond dispute, but the information available to the public and the form in which it is reproduced can mislead. Statistics of crime are always likely to increase for a number of reasons; a larger and more mixed population; improved and more uniform methods of recording; the need to report crime before initiating an insurance claim and so on. A great deal of recorded crime is comparatively trivial and no one has any idea how much crime goes or, in the past, has gone unrecorded. Violent crime, however, is another matter. A very high proportion of crimes involving violence against the person are cleared up for obvious reasons: the concentration of police effort on matters so likely to cause public concern and the fact that in about half of them the identity of the assailant is known. The real problem emerging from the statistical fog is the significant increase in selective crimes of violence: of planned robbery and burglary directed at particular targets, and in which firearms or other weapons are carried. The number of the latter is still not large in comparison with, for example, the United States, but the trend is worrying because it suggests that professional criminals are becoming aware of the limitations of the police and the system of criminal justice; that such crime can, in fact, be highly rewarding. The professional burglar or robber in this country has a six out of ten chance of escaping arrest (though this will obviously diminish as he repeats his offences); and if and when he is caught a four out of ten chance of acquittal. The odds are even more in his favour in America where only one in five of those who commit serious crime is arrested and only one in twelve convicted.

In this country, however, this disturbing trend has a counterbalance which is too often overlooked. Never has a citizen been better able to offset so widely losses arising from crime. There is not, of course, any adequate consolation for the effect on some of the victims of violence or even of those who find their homes burgled and their property destroyed, but it is only right to point out that never in our history has the loss from crime been so widely replaced or lessened by private insurance or by the benefits of the welfare state. Theft losses reported by insurers rose from £34 million in 1964 to £62 million in 1969 and to £100 million in 1974. Even the effect of personal violence is to some extent softened by the Criminal Injuries Compensation Board, which, by 1975, had paid out more than £24 million since it was established in 1964.

The understandable doubts and misgivings provoked by what is loosely called 'the permissive society' and emotional reaction to reports of criminal violence – murder, sexual and other assaults, robbery and burglary – tend to obscure the less newsworthy but happier aspects of inevitable social change. A society which has begun to regard human life as more valuable than property has surely made progress? Though there are still manifest inequalities it can hardly be disputed that there is less poverty, that more people have greater opportunities, that social issues evoke a wider response. The growing realisation that there are objectives for criminal justice more important and constructive than mere punishment is surely an indication of change for the better? Irritation caused by the excessive preoccupation of the news and entertainment media with sex and drugs ought surely not to be allowed to colour our view of a society which is unquestionably more tolerant and more healthy than ever before.

It is surely not without significance in that context that the increase in crime has not led to any inordinate increase in police resources, still very small indeed in relation to population, or to any major change in a system of criminal justice which would make it easier to convict the wrongdoer.

Successive governments without exception since the last war have wisely been inclined to favour a cautious and gradual approach to the various remedies thought appropriate to this problem. These include, for example, a streamlining of police organisation by greatly reducing the number of forces; a considerable improvement in technical equipment, including cars, personal radios and computers; an increase in civilian employees and auxiliaries. There has been, too, an attempt to bring the law more up to date and in keeping with contemporary thought and to achieve, so far as is proper, a greater uniformity in enforcement of the more common offences. But there has been no attempt to increase police resources beyond the minimum thought appropriate to maintain a reasonable degree of public confidence. And most significant of all, there has been no attempt to achieve greater effectiveness by increasing the powers of the police under the law.

The same approach can be seen in the reaction of society to the second category of violence we are considering, that arising from social conditions, political demonstrations, trade disputes and so on. In considering this it is essential to understand the difference between law enforcement in Great Britain and many other countries.

The police here have never been, as in other countries, an executive arm of the government. We are not, as is the case in many countries, subject to orders from central or local government, from ministers or officials. We are paid to discharge the responsibility of each local community to keep the peace and in doing so we exercise a personal authority which cannot be widened or restricted by anyone but Parliament. We are accountable for our actions to the law itself, both criminal and civil, to local police authorities, to the central government and ultimately to public opinion. A chief officer of police can be sued for damages in respect of the action of an unidentified junior. The small number of police, our lack of offensive equipment, our limited powers and our accountability locally and centrally all demonstrate our subservience to, rather than mastery of, the public. These factors undoubtedly affect the actions or policies of the police in dealing with social violence. In the last resort, in the more serious cases, a jury drawn from our fellow citizens will judge the rightness of our action.

The law goes farther than this to deny the social agitator a sense of oppression. The right to demonstrate or to picket is recognised and the duty of the police may properly include the protection of both demonstrators and pickets. Damage to property during a riot may be made good by the local police authority and criminal injury may be compensated by the Criminal Injuries Compensation Board.

It is against that background that you should consider whether social violence has increased in this country or whether that is an illusion created, even if unintentionally, by newspapers and television. Violence has always been a natural aspect of society and, indeed, many social changes now regarded as wholly acceptable have been achieved by it. Local self-government, social legislation and parliamentary reform all owe something to social violence. The trade unions did not emerge without it. The Chartist movement between 1837 and 1848 laid the foundation of what we now regard as constitutional democracy. The suffragette movement between 1905 and 1914 resorted to violence to a degree now largely forgotten or unremarked. There was violence during the General Strike and during the hunger marches of the thirties: but violence has tended to diminish as the claims which inspired it have been conceded.

The post-war trend of passive disobedience demonstrated by the Committee of 100 and the Campaign for Nuclear Disarmament gave way for a time to more active and occasionally violent action in support of such issues as Vietnam, racial discrimination and university reform, but these have not so far achieved the degree of popular support necessary to pose major problems, possibly because they relate to causes less basic than universal franchise and the right to negotiate conditions of employment collectively. There is really nothing new in current expressions of dissent, including squatting, sit-ins, demos and even the occasional and traditionally unsuccessful home-made bomb, but increasingly they reflect a wider awareness of issues often not related to our own society but to mankind in general. Improvement in education, wider communication by newspaper, television and radio, easier and cheaper travel, all this allows and encourages people to question custom and precedent, to form their own opinions and to reject decisions on moral issues made by the majority – and perhaps a small majority – of those elected to represent them in the legislature. It also enables them to be better informed about the actions of government at every level. This development has happily been matched by a growing realisation that suppression and force are not good methods of opposing change in a free society, except in wholly exceptional circumstances likely to command the overwhelming approval of the people.

Attempts to achieve political objectives by coercion or violence are, of course, unlawful and in a sophisticated society ought to be unnecessary but to counter them by excessive violence may in practice go far to help militants to achieve their aims or allow them a degree of public sympathy or support which they would not otherwise receive. The police therefore, both as a matter of law and of strategy, adhere strictly to the doctrine of minimum force, notwithstanding that this may involve acceptance of minor casualties and harassment. This does not, of course, imply willingness to allow militant demonstrators their way, but to deny them success by the least violent means. The courts, constitutionally free from interference by the government and possibly because of their satisfaction at their ability to demonstrate that freedom, have long applied the same policy and are careful not to make martyrs in political or pseudo-political causes. It may be argued that this policy carried too far provokes an occasional need for exemplary severity, of which the sentences in the Notting Hill and Cambridge Garden House Hotel disorders are good examples; or that it encourages a preference for expediency rather than the strict letter of the law, as in the abandonment under pressure of the South African cricket tour. These are certainly debatable points. In a free society such as ours, government must be by consent. The forcible suppression of a minority, whether it be the extreme right, the conventional left or the new left, except in time of war, is the negation of freedom and can only be achieved by overwhelming resources of manpower willing to enforce undemocratic laws. No such resources or law exist here; nor would they be politically acceptable.

I have touched briefly on the police role and their dependence on popular approval for the limited degree of effectiveness expected of them. The army is an even less effective instrument for police purposes in the homeland and not primarily because of its smallness or its other commitments. Since the early nineteenth century there has been a growing distaste on the part of both army and people for the involvement of troops in the homeland in a peace-keeping role, and this has become traditional. The purpose, equipment, training, command structure and accountability of soldiers can hardly be said to be so clearly related to the concept of government by consent as are those of the civil police. They represent, as General Hackett pointed out, the ultimate sanction available to the government. It is important to appreciate that notwithstanding the effects of group loyalty and discipline, both army and police reflect contemporary society. Neither would be likely to give unthinking obedience to policies they considered oppressive or inhuman. The simple truth is that there is not today any force in Great Britain capable of maintaining indefinitely a government not enjoying the support or the tolerance of the overwhelming majority of the people. There is no doubt that this is a potent factor in determining the attitude of the government, the courts and the police to political demonstrations; indeed of demonstrators, protesters and the public generally. You may regard this as an admission of weakness. In fact, it is the opposite. Notwithstanding our economic difficulties and other internal problems, it is unlikely that society in Great Britain has ever been more stable and secure from internal threat than it is today; a security derived not from force or from power but from flexibility, compromise and reason commanding general approval.

My comments so far have clearly related only to Great Britain. This is because I have only superficial knowledge of social conditions in other countries. I think it obvious that social violence is inseparable from the political, economic or other conditions in which it occurs. But the lessons or conclusions to be drawn from the experience of any sophisticated society can surely have some relevance to other comparable social conditions or for emergent and less socially developed countries. You will have noticed, I expect, that I have not touched upon a third category of social violence, namely, attempts to change or usurp the role of government or constitution by force. That is because modern English history, unlike that of many other nations, offers no example for such a trend.

Those among you with personal experience of it may feel that I have evaded the issue of Northern Ireland. The situation there is that since the Province was founded fifty years ago it has never enjoyed government by consent in the sense that the remainder of the United Kingdom understands that phrase. The Cameron Report on the cause of disorders in Northern Ireland lists in detail the reasons for the unacceptability of the Northern Ireland government to a significant and increasing minority of the electorate. The report by Lord Hunt and his colleagues outlined the difficulties of the police in attempting to keep the peace in a community torn by sectarian strife. The real problem is how to prevent fighting, disorder and mindless violence during the time necessary to satisfy the minority of the government's intention to implement the various reforms it has undertaken and to convince those who oppose them that they are essential to the democratic way of life. This cannot be achieved by an unarmed police force of 5,000 men in a community of $1\frac{1}{2}$ million and the preservation of order by the use of minimum force has necessarily fallen to the lot of the army.

The situation illustrates only too well the point I am trying to make in this talk, that the methods to be adopted in keeping the peace will inevitably reflect the historical, constitutional and political conditions of the community. Unarmed London policemen would be as unlikely to meet the needs of Berlin, Chicago or Hong Kong as the CRS, the Bereitschaftspolizei or the Japanese Riot Police would be acceptable to the people of our metropolis. But the police methods used in

London surely suggest a constitutional and political stability that alone makes them appropriate.

What conclusions, if any, can we draw from the points I have made so far? Do we, do you think, live in a more violent world? Do events in Northern Ireland, Pakistan, the Middle East, Cyprus, Algeria, Czechoslovakia, Hungary and Vietnam in the post-war period alone suggest a discernible change in human behaviour? There is continual subversion and periodic revolt in different countries and continents which inevitably give the impression of a world in ferment. I doubt whether even a speculative answer to those questions can have any real value, but of two conclusions we can be quite sure. The first is the greater sophistication and striking power of the violent inspired by political motives. The second is the certainty that it will attract public attention on a scale undreamed of by earlier generations. Newspapers, radio and, above all, television have made violence a cause for concern to millions irrespective of the country in which it occurs. The words Sharpeville, Chicago riots, Belfast and My Lai have acquired a meaning they never had before. The hijacking of an aircraft for a political cause captures the attention of the whole literate world. Perhaps the most worrying aspect of the present situation is not so much the use of violence itself as the extent to which it can be used intentionally or unintentionally to create an emotional imbalance in the minds of the watching or listening millions. The best-intentioned television producer or director does not always accomplish the admittedly difficult feat of setting the newsworthy in the context of the ordinary. It is not so much that the public see on their television screens incidents which are not factual. It is simply that they can almost never be in context. In a free society we believe in a free press, including television, but freedom without responsibility can be as harmful as repression. Somehow, in some way yet undevised, those who control and operate our news media must ensure that its primary purpose in matters of social well-being should be to inform and not to entertain; and by 'entertain' I mean to reproduce factual incidents without due regard to the context in which they occurred.

For those of us actively involved in the containment of violence, whether at home or abroad, there is only one conclusion we can safely draw: it is that our role is never likely to diminish in importance. Few, if any, countries can these days exist in isolation. Each, with or without external influence, will find, by force if necessary, its own level of internal stability based on the considerations which sooner or later must affect all societies. If the balance of terror represented by nuclear weapons lessens the prospect of world warfare, it nevertheless speeds the process of mutual involvement for the nations living under it. This must give rise to a movement towards a common level in political, economic and social affairs, a movement in which I have tried to persuade you, violence is inherent. It is our task to control and contain it and it is therefore necessary for us to see it objectively and above all without the emotion that violence so easily arouses. Many of you will by now have come to the conclusion that Edward Gibbon has said all this before. So indeed he did: but in about six volumes as compared with some dozen pages!

7

The Metropolitan Police and Political Demonstrations*

On such evidence as I have seen there may well be good reason to wonder whether magistrates do always appreciate the gravity of an offence against public order. Abuse of liberty endangers liberty itself; it is a serious offence to depreciate the currency of freedom by resorting to violence and public disorder.

Lord Justice Scarman

The maintenance of order during political demonstrations has always been the most sensitive problem of the Metropolitan Police. The need to control the London mob without recourse to the army was, in fact, one of the strongest reasons for the creation of the force in 1829. Though each decade has produced its succession of problems we have never departed from the basic doctrine of minimum force, although improved communications have made possible more sophisticated and flexible methods of control and containment. It is surprising that political demonstrations throughout almost a century and a half have resulted in few serious casualties. The gathering of crowds to give violent expression to their views, a common feature of the late

* Lecture given at the National Police College, Bramshill, in 1974.

eighteenth and most of the nineteenth centuries, has given way to a now well-established tradition of comparatively orderly demonstrations marred only occasionally by violence, even then usually initiated by, and confined to, minority groups.

Appendix A gives general statistics relating to demonstrations in the Metropolitan Police District in 1972, 1973 and 1974, while in view of the public interest aroused in the demonstrations centred on Red Lion Square on 15 June 1974, which became the subject of the recent public inquiry under the chairmanship of Lord Justice Scarman, Appendix D gives separate details in relation to the events of that day. The total number of political demonstrations in London during 1972, 1973 and 1974 was 1,321. Only 54 of these demonstrations involved disorder resulting in a total of 623 arrests. In these three years 297 police officers, 49 persons who were arrested and 27 other participants were reported to have been injured, none fatally until Red Lion Square. However, not every civilian participant will report minor injury and there cannot, therefore, be any true record of all casualties. The figures nevertheless suggest an avoidance of extreme violence and a tradition of containment of activities which, though usually lawful, are often controversial, sometimes provocative and occasionally open to exploitation and misrepresentation and which are frequently the cause of inconvenience to the public.

The years since 1945 have not been without their major issues for political demonstrations. Suez, the visit of Queen Frederika, Ban the Bomb, the Committee of 100, the Vietnam War and Stop the '70 Tour in their differing contexts are evocative words in the history of London political demonstrations. The violence arising from demonstrations in support of some of these issues was sometimes extensive. Any political cause or event, sometimes in lands far away, can produce demonstrations on the streets of London at very short notice and there has emerged a questionable tradition that the right to pursue that activity shall over-ride all other considerations. The reported massacre at Wiriyamu in Portuguese Africa, the visit of the then prime minister of Portugal and the invasion of Cyprus are recent examples of this.

It is not possible to attribute to any one factor the general avoidance of extreme disorder and the comparative rarity of serious casualties in so long a history of political demonstrations. The underlying reason is perhaps our longstanding tradition of changing governments without bloodshed or tumult and a freedom of expression unsurpassed elsewhere. This has allowed a unique relationship between the people and the police, who traditionally depend on goodwill rather than force in carrying out their duties. Of the more immediate reasons for the avoidance of serious disorder and casualties, perhaps the most obvious is an adequate police presence and a lack of weaponry. The police have never had any special weapons or equipment for crowd control. We rely on manpower, supported by horses where necessary, as the most effective and least harmful means of control, and we have nothing more lethal than a wooden truncheon on which to rely in emergencies. Similarly, demonstrators in this country rarely have recourse to lethal weapons, possession of which is, in any case, in many circumstances an offence involving liability to arrest. There is usually no intentional separation of police and demonstrators. The one group escorts the other when walking in procession and even when facing each other outside an embassy or police station they are usually within touching distance, their mutual vulnerability being more evident than if seen at a distance.

Although the support of the public at large for police aims and methods is a major factor in keeping down the temperature at demonstrations and minimising casualties, the lack of fatal and serious casualties has allowed unjustified complacency in the public attitude to political demonstrations. These are occasionally both violent and frightening and there has emerged a small minority of extremist causes whose adherents leave no doubt of their belief in the use of force and lack of scruple to further political aims. That these groups are contained without more serious consequences is in the main due to the fortitude, the training and the tolerance of the police and the inhibitions natural to their role. The limitation of police powers in dealing with demonstrations and demonstrators, the accountability of the police and their constant exposure to the news media and to parliamentary questions, and not least the fact that police have learnt from experience that in the long run restraint is usually the most effective way to preserve order and maintain control; all these factors have the effect of creating an unwillingness to abandon persuasion except as a last resort. This unwillingness has perhaps been reinforced over the years by growing police awareness of the tolerance of the courts in dealing with those found guilty of an offence.

Appendix B shows the outcome of prosecutions arising from demonstrations in 1972, 1973, and 1974 and Appendix C gives details of fines imposed. Appendixes E and F give separate details of the outcome of prosecutions and fines imposed as a result of the events in Red Lion Square on 15 June 1974. During 1972, in only 12 of 231 proved cases of threatening behaviour, assault on police, obstruction of police and of the highway, possessing offensive weapons and criminal damage did a court actually impose a prison sentence, none longer than three months. In 1973 not one of 84 proved cases resulted in a sentence of imprisonment that was not suspended; 17 of these cases were of assault on police and 10 of obstruction, which in practice is usually an attempt to liberate a prisoner. During 1974, notwithstanding an increase in violence and arrests, only 19 of 278 proved cases resulted in prison sentences, 13 of them suspended and none of the remaining six longer than three months.

The level of fines has generally been very low. Perhaps in some cases that is appropriate but there have been many in which convictions for violence have attracted derisory penalties of £10 or so. In mid-1974 that sum was the equivalent of £1·60 in the values of 1936 when the Public Order Act was passed. From the administrative point of view it could be argued that in present circumstances prosecutions involve a waste of scarce and expensive police manpower for no worthwhile result and that in London they could, without disadvantage, be abandoned except in very serious cases intended for the higher courts, such as unlawful assembly or riot.

It is perhaps hardly surprising that in London the police feel that in controlling demonstrations they are at their most vulnerable. Contrary to popular belief, recourse to the courts is sometimes as much an ordeal for the policeman as for the demonstrator and the likelihood of achieving a result of value as a deterrent is clearly remote. The charges are usually contested and the hearing may, therefore, take place long after the event, when the circumstances which gave rise to the demonstration are forgotten or no longer of public interest. The use of force will always attract extensive press and television coverage and ensure complaints against the police by persons involved in actual incidents and by others inspired by a variety of motives. So much is this reaction an accepted part of the demonstration formula that for all major events a complaints officer is designated as a routine measure. All those wishing to complain are directed to him to ensure their uniform and effective reception.

There is, therefore, a profound difference between the attitude of the Metroplitan Police to demonstrations and that attributed to them by political activists who assume that the police act on behalf of the government of the day, that they will readily resort to the use of force, that they are a corporate body sympathising with the right rather than the left, that the courts are prejudiced in their favour and that they are virtually unaccountable for their behaviour when controlling demonstrations. Some of these beliefs may be prompted by folk memories, true or untrue, of the thirties. There is not, however, any foundation for them today.

Though its administration is subject to government approval, the Metropolitan force, like provincial forces, is free from political interference in operational matters. We regard political demonstrations of every kind primarily with resignation, albeit a weary tolerance. Far from there being a sympathy for any particular party, any departure from reasonably orderly behaviour, whether by adherents of the right, the centre or the left, is regarded by most London policemen with equal distaste. We do, of course, recognise that demonstrations are to be preferred to many other methods of protest, but our generally resigned and apprehensive approach to these events is hardly surprising once it is realised that an excess of fervour and extremist views can produce controversy, complaints, unreason, violence and lies in circumstances in which it is usually impossible to expose the truth and in which the police are often in the middle.

The courts, the press and the public probably do not appreciate the sophistication with which the extremist uses political demonstrations to undermine confidence in established institutions. The planned counter-demonstration, the use of deliberate violence, the routine complaints of police brutality, the ready spokesman without evidence or conscience, all these constitute a technique with which London police are all too familiar. Like Lord Justice Scarman, I do not doubt the sincerity of their feelings, but I am under no illusion about the lengths to which they are prepared to go. These are perhaps seen at their best by a letter printed in a national newspaper of 19 June in which the writer eloquently, persuasively, more in sorrow than in anger, commented adversely as an eyewitness on police behaviour at Red Lion Square. Readers were not to know that the signature at its foot should have been that of Paul Josef Goebbels since the letter was in the best tradition of the unscrupulous political propagandist. Inquiry showed that no such person as the signatory lived at the address from which the letter purported to come. Ironically the deception was only revealed because it was conscientiously investigated as a complaint against the police.

The policeman does not, as is sometimes suggested, welcome a possible confrontation with extremist demonstrators. He knows that his behaviour will be scrutinised closely, that the rules governing his conduct are more strict than those applicable to the demonstrators and the consequences for him are potentially more disadvantageous. In short he feels apprehension rather than enthusiasm at involvement in a situation from which he expects nothing but trouble. His every instinct, when trying to keep rival factions apart, is to let them fight it out and to clean up the mess, but his sense of duty persuades him that the public interest requires the prevention or containment of disorder no matter what the risks or adverse consequences for him.

Political demonstrations seem to give satisfaction in the main to those taking part. The public as a whole are usually not interested unless affected by inconvenience or aroused by disorder and violence. Nevertheless, the right to hold them is much valued and jealously preserved. In the event of violence there is usually much comment on the extent to which the police exercised or failed to exercise control. Speculation as to whether the police should have prohibited or regulated a political demonstration usually betrays a lack of knowledge of the law or of the difficulties of applying it. No useful purpose is achieved by prohibitions or regulations incapable of enforcement, or in respect of which judicial penalties are likely to be slight. Demonstrators who can rely on massive support, such as the Committee of 100 in the 1960s, are unlikely to be deterred by such restrictions, and political extremists are likely to welcome them. For both, disregard or defiance is sure to achieve maximum publicity at very little cost.

Almost all prosecutions arising from public demonstrations are tried in courts of summary jurisdiction in which penalties, in the event of conviction, are limited. There is a marked contrast between the chaotic violence of a demonstration, at which a faction has been determined at all costs to provoke police reaction, to prevent the public expression of an opinion to which its members are opposed or to penetrate to a symbolic target such as an embassy, and the quiet and ordered atmosphere of a court days or weeks later. A note by the solicitor to the Metropolitan Police of the current legislation and common law relating to the offences most commonly committed in the course of demonstrations is attached at Appendix G for easy reference. Appendixes B and C, showing the outcome of the prosecutions in 1972, 1973 and 1974 indicate that even the limited maxima available to the justices are rarely applied. Mistakenly or not, the police believe that this results from magisterial unawareness of, or disagreement with, the Court of Appeal's answer to the defence of 'Why pick on me?' frequently put forward by demonstrators plucked from among their fellows and brought before the courts.

The relevant part of the judgement of the Court of Appeal in what is known as the Garden House case is as follows:

'The next point to be mentioned is what might be called the "Why pick on me?" argument. It has been suggested that there is something wrong in giving an appropriate sentence to one convicted of an offence because there are considerable numbers of others who were at the same time committing the same offence, some of whom indeed, if identified and arrested and established as having taken a more serious part, could have received heavier sentences. This is a plea which is almost invariably put forward where the offence is one of those classed as disturbances of the public peace – such as riots, unlawful assemblies and affrays. It indicates a failure to appreciate that on these confused and tumultuous occasions each individual who takes an active part by deed or encouragement is guilty of a really grave offence by being one of the number engaged in a crime against the peace. It is, moreover, impracticable for a small number of police when sought to be overwhelmed by a crowd to make a large number of arrests. . . . If this plea were acceded to, it would reinforce that feeling which may undoubtedly exist that if an offender is but one of a number he is unlikely to be picked on, or even if he is so picked upon, can escape proper punishment because others were not arrested at the same time. Those who choose to take part in such unlawful occasions must do so at their peril. . . . In the view of this Court, it is a wholly wrong approach to take the acts of any individual participator in isolation. They were not committed in isolation and, as already indicated, it is that very fact that constitutes the gravity of the offence.'

When considering what action to take in respect of the declared intention to hold extremist demonstrations in support of any political persuasion, police observe scrupulously the principle declared to the House of Commons by a former Home Secretary:

'If this is indeed a free country and we are free people, a man is just as much entitled to profess the Fascist philosophy as any other, and he is perfectly entitled to proclaim it and expound it so long as he does not exceed the reasonable bounds which are set by law.'

Most political demonstrations pose problems no worse than those arising from inconvenience to public and police. There is adequate liaison between the organisers and the police and differences of opinion about routes, timing and so on are usually resolved amicably. By contrast, a small number of demonstrations present severe problems. Occasionally the organisers refuse to disclose details of their plans, or reveal a plan to which police object on grounds of inconvenience to the public or possible disorder, without eventual agreement being possible. Minority extremist groups joining demonstrations organised by much larger groups sometimes fail to disclose an intention to depart from arrangements agreed by the organisers with the police. Sometimes demonstrations are mounted at very short notice leaving insufficient time to agree arrangements or to brief all those taking part. Difficulties of this kind, as well as our own administrative problems, require the maintenance of a special department at New Scotland Yard to ensure a continuity of experience and uniformity of judgement always available to divisional commanders.

The Metropolitan Police have always been disinclined to seek the approval of the Secretary of State for an Order prohibiting political processions for a specified period on the grounds that this encourages extremist minority groups to threaten violence with the object of achieving the suppression of opposition opinion. We believe that attempts by coercion or force to suppress free speech are not only wrong but unlawful and that behaviour of that kind must be resisted no matter what the inconvenience or cost. To give way to such threats is not just to defer to mob rule but to encourage it.

The regulation of political demonstrations to reduce or rule out provocation and possible conflict is quite another matter. This can be both proper and necessary but success must depend upon the adequacy of police manpower, the skill and determination of police leadership and in the last resort the willingness to meet force with force. The courts are unlikely to impose sentences that will have a practical deterrent effect, save in really exceptional cases, such as the Notting Hill and Garden House riots. It is arguable, too, that the police, discouraged by apparent magisterial tolerance of unlawful violence by demonstrators and weary of harassment by complainants, journalists and political movements alike, have themselves been inclined to show excessive tolerance. Time after time they have remained passive in the face of missiles and physical assault, particularly in Grosvenor Square and Whitehall. They have done so not only because they recognise the dangers of open conflict but also because they are loath to invite the torrent of complaint and criticism sure to be provoked by more vigorous self-defence, however justified. Certainly the extremist minority groups these days show no sense of apprehension in threatening or actually assaulting police. But if the use of force by police officers appears to be the only way of securing the Queen's Peace it is plainly the duty of the police to use, or to authorise the use of, such force as is needed and is lawful, and not to be inhibited from doing so either by the fact that the aims of the demonstrators are political or by the inevitable claim that any force used by the police is brutality.

The problem is, however, less one of the willingness and ability of police to contain violent extremists than of social attitudes. Extremist demonstrators see nothing improper in intimidating political opponents by threats of violence. They regard actual violence in pursuit of that objective as justifiable and any counter-action by the police as provocative or worse. The public and, indeed, the courts, are so used to hearing this point of view that it does not arouse the reaction it deserves. Conduct that would provoke widespread condemnation in a football hooligan is condoned in a political demonstrator. To the police, the difference is difficult to discern. We alone bear the brunt of it and no one has in recent years done more than render lip service to our predicament. It is an interesting reflection of current attitudes that shoplifting in London should be punished more severely than violence in pursuit of political activities. Failure to persuade society of the need to view misbehaviour at political demonstrations in London with more positive disapproval will inevitably provoke demands for more severe punishment and control by permits or licences, hitherto regarded as unnecessary in this country. The former would be likely to create martyrs and the latter would involve the police in a highly undesirable process of appearing to approve or disapprove of political activities. Measures of that kind should, in any case, be unnecessary if the full weight of public opinion can be brought to bear on the problem.

The press can do most to lessen unlawful violence by giving it the publicity and disapproval it deserves and by focusing attention on court proceedings arising from it. It is, after all, public opinion to which political activists are most sensitive. The militant extremists who used violence in some of the industrial disputes of 1972, abusing the legal and traditional rights acquired by strikers over many years of industrial conflict, though not at all daunted by the police or the courts, did not make the mistake in 1974 of risking adverse public reaction with a general election in the offing.

It is no less essential for the police to have public opinion behind them. This can only be done by impeccable behaviour, by open administration and by facilitating the widest possible press coverage before, during and after events. Public opinion, if sufficiently strong, can sway courts and politicians and, indeed, can influence the behaviour even of the political extremist. It can also exercise a salutary restraint upon the police themselves while reinforcing our determination not to allow inconvenience, criticism, abuse and personal injury to deter us from upholding the public interest.

We shall continue to uphold freedom on the streets of London whatever the cost to us in danger, physical injury, libel and slander because that is one of the causes to which we the police are dedicated and we shall hope by our conduct to deserve and achieve in that task the support and understanding of the press, the public and of the courts who alone have the power to determine whether our efforts will succeed or fail and whose decisions are, therefore, as important for the public as they are for us.

Appendix A: General Statistics Relating to Demonstrations in the Metropolitan Police District in the Years 1972, 1973 and 1974

In 1972, 1973 and 1974 there were respectively 470, 445 and 406 major events requiring special police arrangements, making a total of 1,321 during the three-year period.

Of the 1,321 events:

(a) 703 were not the subject of any subsequent report by local police, being both small and orderly,

(b) 411 were handled by local divisions without an Operation Order being issued from New Scotland Yard. These events involved a total of 42,000 police officers,

(c) 207 were covered by 96 Operation Orders. These events involved a total of 63,000 police officers. The figures in the Summary Table show that there was proportionately a heavy increase in the number of events covered by Operation Orders in 1974 compared with the two previous years.

Disorder occurred in 54 of these events and a total of 623 arrests were made; 740 charges were preferred and 18 juveniles cautioned.

Summary Table

	1972	1973	1974	Total for three-year period
Total events:	470	445	406	1,321
(a) no subsequent report	253	256	194	703
(b) handled locally – no Operation Order	163	123	125	411
(c) covered by Operation Order	54	66	87	207
(no. of Operation Orders issued)	(28)	(26)	(42)	(96)
Police manpower involved:				
(b) handled locally – no Operation Order	17,300	9,400	15,100	41,800
(c) covered by Operation Order	19,300	17,700	26,400	63,400
Number of events involving disorder	15	19	20	54
Number of arrests made	239	78	306	623
Number of injuries reported:	200	47	126*	373*
(i) to police officers	161	34	102	297
(ii) to persons who were arrested	24	8	17	49
(iii) to other participants	15	5	7*	27*

* Including one fatal injury.

Appendix B: Results of Cases Brought Against 623 Persons Arrested During Demonstrations in the Metropolitan Police District in the Years 1972, 1973 and 1974

Charge	Total offences	Proceedings completed	Cases dismissed	Cautions to juveniles	Total convictions	Convictions			
						Absolute/ conditional discharge, bound over	Fine	Suspended sentence	Imprisonment
Threatening or insulting words or behaviour	234	232	42	5	185	49	126	5	5
Assault on police	148	136	30	1	105	12	58	25	10
Obstructing police	102	96	16	5	75	14	60	1	–
Possession of offensive weapons	34	32	7	–	25	6	15	1	3
Obstruction of the highway	148	146	12	6	128	9	119	–	–
Criminal damage	15	15	2	–	13	1	12	–	–
Other offences	77	53	8	1	44	–	41	3	–
TOTALS	758	710*	117	18	575	91	431	35	18†

* At the end of 1974 there were 48 cases in respect of which proceedings had not been completed. In 27 of these cases warrants had been issued in respect of defendants who had failed to appear.

† Of the 18 prison sentences 12 were for one month, 2 for two months (both for assault on police) and 4 for three months (3 of them for assault on police).

Appendix C: Details of Fines Imposed Following the Conviction of Persons Arrested During Demonstrations in the Metropolitan Police District in the Years 1972, 1973 and 1974

Charge	Number of fines imposed	Amounts of fines							Average fine	Maximum fine
		£5 or less	£6–£10	£11–£15	£16–£20	£21–£25	£26–£30	Over £30		
Threatening or insulting words or behaviour	126	19	47	24	15	7	8	6	£15	£100
Assault on police	58	1	11	6	16	6	5	13	£24	£100
Obstructing police	60	16	28	5	11	—	—	—	£11	£20
Possession of offensive weapon	15	—	6	—	3	5	—	1	£20	£200
Obstruction of the highway	119	86	22	10	1	—	—	—	£7	£50
Criminal damage	12	5	5	—	1	—	1	—	£9	£400
TOTALS	390	127	119	45	47	18	14	20		

Appendix D: Statistics Relating to Demonstrations Centred on Red Lion Square on 15 June 1974

Number of demonstrators in National Front march	900
Number of counter-demonstrators in 'Liberation' march	1,000
Total number of demonstrators	1,900

Police manpower involved:	
Uniformed foot officers	711
Mounted officers	25
Support officers	122
Traffic Division officers	35
CID officers	30
Total from all ranks and branches	923

Number of arrests made	51

Number of injuries reported	54*
(i) to police officers	46
(ii) to persons who were arrested	5
(iii) to other participants	3*

* Including one fatal injury.

Appendix E: Results of Charges Brought Against 51 Persons Arrested During Demonstrations Centred on Red Lion Square on 15 June 1974

Charge	Total charges	Proceedings completed	Charges dismissed	Convictions Total convictions	Convictions Absolute/conditional discharge, bound over	Convictions Fine	Convictions Suspended sentence	Convictions No separate penalty
Threatening or insulting words or behaviour	30	30	10	20	6	13	—	1
Assault on police	32	32	14	18	3	12	3	—
Obstructing police	14	14	2	12	2	9	—	1
Possession of offensive weapon	5	5	2	3	1	2	—	—
Criminal damage	1	1	1	—	—	—	—	—
TOTAL	82	82	29	53	12	36	3*	2

* Of the 3 suspended sentences, 1 was for three months' imprisonment suspended for two years, 1 for four months suspended for a year and 1 for three months suspended for a year; the last two of these sentences were suspended on appeal. In fact, therefore, no one served a sentence of imprisonment.

Appendix F: Details of Fines Imposed Following the Conviction of Persons Arrested During Demonstrations Centred on Red Lion Square on 15 June 1974

Charge	Number of fines imposed	Amounts of fines							Average fine	Highest fine imposed	Maximum fine	Legal aid costs awarded	Costs awarded
		£5 or less	£6–£10	£11–£15	£16–£20	£21–£25	£26–£30	Over £30					
Threatening or insulting words or behaviour	13	2	5	2	1	1	2	—	£14	£30	£100	4	8
Assaults on police	12	—	2	—	1	2	1	6	£32	£50	£100	3	6
Obstructing police	9	—	5	—	4	—	—	—	£14	£20	£20	3	4
Possession of offensive weapon	2	1	—	1	—	—	—	—	£10	£15	£200	—	—
TOTAL	36	3	12	3	6	3	3	6		£15	£200	10	18

Appendix G: Note of the Current Legislation and Common Law Relating to the Offences Most Commonly Committed in the Course of Demonstrations

Prosecutions in the Metropolitan Police District arising from political demonstrations are usually brought under one or other of the following:

1 Section 4 of the Public Order Act 1936

Having an offensive weapon at a public meeting

SUMMARY TRIAL ONLY – 3 months' imprisonment or £50 fine or both

2 Section 5 of the Public Order Act 1936

Using threatening/abusive/insulting words or behaviour or displaying any such sign

ON SUMMARY TRIAL – 3 months' imprisonment or £100 fine or both

ON INDICTMENT – 12 months' imprisonment or £500 fine or both

3 Section 1 of the Prevention of Crime Act 1953

Having an offensive weapon in a public place

ON SUMMARY TRIAL – 3 months' imprisonment or £200 fine or both

ON INDICTMENT – 2 years' imprisonment or unlimited fine or both

4 Section 51(1) of the Police Act 1964

Assaulting a constable in the execution of his duty

ON SUMMARY TRIAL – 6 months' imprisonment (9 months after previous conviction) or £100 fine or both

		ON INDICTMENT – 2 years' imprisonment or fine or both
5	Section 51(3) of the Police Act 1964	Wilfully obstructing a constable
		SUMMARY TRIAL ONLY – I months' imprisonment or £20 fine or both
6	In unusual circumstances, under section 54(12) of the Metropolitan Police Act 1839	Using indecent language SUMMARY TRIAL ONLY – £20 fine
7	In unusual circumstances, under Section 54 (13) of the Metropolitan Police Act 1839	Using threatening, abusive or insulting words or behaviour SUMMARY TRIAL ONLY – £20 fine

In exceptional cases, for example the Bloody Sunday Irish Demonstration or the Notting Hill Anti-Police March:

8	Causing an affray	
9	Taking part in a riot	
10	Unlawful assembly	
11	Conspiracies to commit 8, 9 and 10 and conspiracies to commit a public mischief or to trespass (subject to the decision in Kamara v. DPP)	8, 9, 10 and 11 are *all* COMMON LAW INDICTABLE OFFENCES – imprisonment and/or fine with no limitation on either

Appendix H: The Red Lion Square Disorders of 15 June 1974. Extracts from the Report of Inquiry by The Rt Hon. Lord Justice Scarman, OBE*

6. This inquiry has been concerned to discover where the balance should be struck, and the role of the police in maintaining it. Indiscipline amongst demonstrators, heavy-handed police reaction to disorder are equally mischievous: for each can upset the balance. Violent demonstrators by creating public disorder infringe a fundamental human right which belongs to the rest of us: excessively violent police reaction to public disorder infringes the rights of the protesters. The one and the other are an affront to civilised living.

THE ROLE OF THE POLICE

7. The police are not to be required in any circumstances to exercise political judgement. Their role is the maintenance of public order – no more, and no less. When the National Front marches, the police have no concern with their political message; they will intervene only if the circumstances are such that a breach of the peace is reasonably apprehended. Even if the message be 'racist', it is not for the police to 'ban the march' or compel it to disperse unless public order is threatened. If, of course, the message appears to infringe the race relations legislation, the police have a duty to report the facts so that consideration may be given to subsequent prosecution: moreover in such circumstances a senior police officer, accompanying the march, might think it wise to warn the organisers of the march that, if it proceeds with its slogans, he will report the fact. But it is vital, if the police are to be kept out of political controversy, that in a public order situation their sole immediate concern is, and is seen to be, with public order.

29. Mr Gerrard, the Deputy Assistant Commissioner in charge of the operation, was in the square and saw what was

* *Crown copyright. Reproduced by permission of the Controller of HMSO from Cmnd. 5919.*

happening. He decided to bring forward the mounted police in support of the foot police cordon and for a time the horsemen added the weight of their horses in support of the foot police line. Two units of the Special Patrol Group (SPG) were also summoned from Richbell Place where they had been held in reserve.

53. The mounted police penetrated the centre of the crowd without much difficulty. It was a sudden and unexpected manoeuvre. Some were alarmed, even to the point of panic: others reacted with indignation, as is clear from photographs which show one young man brandishing a stick at a mounted officer, and another seizing hold of a horse's reins. Some mounted officers had drawn their short truncheons; they explained that this was necessary for defensive purposes. The foot police came forward from the centre of the crossroads, and Sergeant Farmery, having obtained authority by radio from Chief Superintendent Adams, led his men into the rear of the crowd in wedge formation towards the mounted officers.

Conduct of the mounted police

74. The deployment of the mounted police against a disorderly crowd will always lead to a certain amount of fright and panic. So it was on this occasion. But there is no evidence that anything serious, in the way of crushing injuries, was done by the horses. When the police cordon was attacked in Red Lion Square there was a considerable amount of noise, and the horses, standing behind the cordon, spun round, but they were quickly brought under control, and so remained throughout the afternoon; indeed the calm of the horses, among the struggling human beings, is a feature of the photographic evidence. I am satisfied that there was never any 'charge' by mounted police in Red Lion Square; the horses never reached a pace faster than a walk, and the pressure on the crowd was moderate and reasonable, though firm. At the Vernon Place crossroads the mounted police entered the crowd at a fast walk, but once they had penetrated used their horses as in Red Lion Square, shepherding the crowd on to the pavements.

75. The mounted police are an invaluable tool for a police force which has decided to manage without riot equipment. They can do what many more foot police officers may take much longer to accomplish, and in a police force which is short of men this is not an unimportant consideration. Their technical effectiveness is shown by the Vernon Place operation where, with the support of the foot police, they succeeded in restoring order within a very short time indeed. Mounted police have been used for crowd control for at least fifty years – one recalls photographs of the famous white horse at the first Wembley cup final – and though their use in dealing with disorder may affront demonstrators (and horse lovers too) they are an irreplaceable police asset. A horse is bigger, can exert more pressure and is less manoeuvrable than the human body of the foot policeman; but how much less formidable it is than the armoured car and water-cannon which are the only alternatives.

76. I find no ground for criticising the control of the horses, or the way they were used; I deal with the use of truncheons by mounted officers separately below.

(b) Mounted police
82. The same rules govern the use of truncheons by mounted police, but their application is different. A mounted policeman carries a long truncheon as well as a short one. None of the police who gave evidence had ever seen the long truncheon used: and it was not used in these disorders. There must be a case for withdrawing it from service: and I would suggest that consideration be given to the possibility of dispensing with it. Mounted police did draw short truncheons in Red Lion Square and Theobold's Road: and I am satisfied that some officers used them. Two questions arise: did they draw them prematurely, in which event the inference would be that they did so to threaten demonstrators rather than to defend themselves? And did they use them for a purpose other than self-defence? It is for the individual policeman to decide when to draw his truncheon: its only legitimate use is self-defence, and each policeman must judge when he personally is threatened. A mounted police-

man may draw his truncheon earlier than one on foot, because, once engaged in the fact of seeking to control a crowd, he has his hands full managing his horse. If he thinks he is going to need his truncheon, he acts sensibly in drawing it before he is committed. I do not, therefore, think it is possible in the circumstances of these disorders to criticise the mounted police for drawing their truncheons before coming into contact with the crowd.

83. It is very much more difficult to reach a judgement as to their use. Powerful though a mounted policeman is, he is at all times very vulnerable: his horse has to be controlled, and his seat kept. Demonstrators were aware of this difficulty and some attempts were made to seize the horses' reins. When this happened, as it did with several officers, it was necessary in self-defence to strike at the demonstrator's arms and hands to force him to let go. Not surprisingly, this was the explanation given by those officers who gave evidence: and, if true, it is a sufficient explanation. A number of demonstrators, however, gave evidence which, if true, meant that, so far from being confined to self-defence, truncheons were used to 'club down' members of the crowd.

84. Only one specific incident was described in any detail. It involved Inspector Fleming who openly admitted striking a demonstrator a glancing blow on the head when he went to the assistance of an officer who was in difficulties. Inspector Fleming properly reported this incident at the time. I accept his explanation that he was acting to defend his colleague and did not aim at the demonstrator's head. The rest of the evidence, when tested in cross-examination, established very little one way or the other. I do not doubt that in the disorders at Red Lion Square and in Theobald's Road some mounted officers did hit some demonstrators with their short truncheons. Some blows may well have landed on the head: but there is no evidence of serious injury.

Reporting failures
86. None of the allegedly violent incidents was considered worthy of report by any of the senior officers present. Nor were there any reports on the returns completed after the

demonstration that any foot police officers had drawn, let alone used their truncheons – though the mounted police were scrupulous in this regard.

93. I think policemen of all ranks were acting reasonably in regarding the crowd as a threat to public order, once some elements of it had mounted the Red Lion Square attack: and I think it difficult to regard as excessive strong measures taken thereafter to maintain public order. Had there been no attack upon the police in Red Lion Square, it would not have been possible, in my judgement, to have justified the movement of the mounted police into the crowd in Theobald's Road or the pursuit and forceful arrests in Boswell Street. But, as it was, in the circumstances of that afternoon, each move was, in my judgement, justified.

111. Mr Cracknell took a risk, the full extent of which at the time he did not realise, when he committed the mounted police, giving them the task of clearing the crowd on to the pavements. The street scene itself provided its own immovable obstacles and dangers (subway entrances and railings), and the police behind presented an obstacle to dispersal. On the other hand, there was a great width of street. In the event no disaster occurred, though no observer liked what he saw, and there was understandable alarm felt by some as the horses entered the crowd. Technically speaking, the operation achieved its objective. It was all over in a few minutes. The crowd was divided into two halves, one pushed to the northern side and the other to the southern side of Theobald's Road. There were some dangerous and frightening moments of pressure near the subway entrances: but the pressure was soon relieved and caused no casualty. Such casualties as occurred arose from scuffles between policemen and individual demonstrators. It is also fair to remember that the police behind the crowd did, in fact, help the operation: they formed a wedge which, linking up with the mounted police, combined to make it a speedy operation, thus helping to shorten the period of danger.

113. If he felt it necessary to use the mounted police, should Mr Cracknell have given a warning (there was a public address apparatus available)? Public order is an

exercise in public relations. It might well have caused less offence and alarm if a warning had been given to the effect that the police required the crowd to disperse. I do not think it would have materially affected the success of the operation: indeed it might have assisted it. I consider that a warning should have been given.

(b) The event

141. The police carried out two major operations on 15 June, the first in Red Lion Square, and the second at the Vernon Place crossroads. The particular point of future importance to be adduced from the first operation is that care must be taken in dispersing a disorderly crowd to ensure that it does not have the opportunity to attack at another vulnerable point. The Vernon Place operation, and the criticisms made of it, confirm that it is important for the officer in charge to ensure, wherever possible, that a crowd has sufficient means of moving away before taking action to disperse or disrupt it. Similarly policemen behind a crowd should bear in mind that their action may be of critical importance to any action taken at the front of the crowd. These are points which could profitably be incorporated in Metropolitan Police training.

142. There are also lessons to be learned in regard to warnings. Current Metropolitan Police thinking seems to be that warnings are ineffective; they frequently attract abuse and are sometimes over-ridden by the noise of the crowd – 'spitting in the wind' as it was described by one police officer. I accept that in a riot situation such as that in Red Lion Square warnings are a waste of time and effort: the police have the immediate duty of restoring order. But the Vernon Place affair was different. Here there was no riot, and the crowd, though it appeared to be hostile and threatening, had not moved to attack either the police or the National Front. A warning could have done no harm; it might have enabled those without violent intent to have left the crowd, and those who remained would not have been able to claim that police action came as a total surprise. There will be some occasions where the police need to keep the element of surprise in order to secure the success of their

operation, and decide for that reason not to give any warning: but this was not the situation at Vernon Place. I think it would be a good general principle that where they propose to take action against a static crowd, the police should first give a warning: only exceptionally should no warning be given.

143. It was suggested to me that the mounted police should be withdrawn from demonstration duty. In my view mounted police are essential, if we are to avoid riot squads and riot equipment, both of which, when they appear, increase tension, alarm, and anger: an illustration of the disastrous effect upon people's minds when the police put on their riot equipment is to be found in what happened in Londonderry on 12 August 1969 at Waterloo Place. The appearance of riot equipment is a sign of trouble ahead but mounted police are as much part of the London scene as the policeman on his beat: and their presence is not an indication of a police intention to resort to force.

144. When used to suppress disorder, mounted police do cause apprehension: but, properly used they do not cause casualties. The proper use of mounted police should be kept under continuous review. If they are to be available for a specific event, one of their senior officers should participate in police planning (this was not done in the planning for Red Lion Square). Normally, they should be used to support foot police: sending them in first, as Mr Cracknell did in Theobald's Road, should be the exception, and is justifiable only if the circumstances are exceptional.

163. I find no ground for criticising the control of the horses of the mounted police, nor the way they were used (paras 74–6).

166. Some foot police officers drew their truncheons, and some officers used them. I do not exclude the possibility of one or two incidents of the misuse of truncheons, but I reject any suggestion of general misuse (para. 81).

167. A number of mounted officers drew their short truncheons. I do not criticise the mounted police for drawing their truncheons before coming into contact with the crowd. I am not prepared to find on the evidence submitted that

the mounted officers misused their truncheons. No officer used or even drew his long truncheon in these disorders; consideration should be given to the possibility of dispensing with it (paras. 82–4).

LESSONS

(a) *Law reform*

181. In my opinion the principle of the law and the balance it strikes between freedom, public order, and the right of passage have not been shown by these disorders to be unsound; and I do not recommend any fundamental reform (para. 124).

182. However the statute law calls for scrutiny. Section 6 of the Race Relations Act 1965 needs radical amendment to make it an effective sanction, particularly I think in relation to its formulation of the intent to be proved before an offence can be established (para. 125).

183. The Commissioner of Police of the Metropolis submitted to my Inquiry that it should be an offence to organise a demonstration without giving prior notice to the police. I do not think the need for this has been established, and I do not recommend this proposed change in the law (paras. 126—8).

184. I recommend that the Public Order Act 1936 be amended to confer upon the senior officer present a power to give a direction as to the route to be followed by a demonstration if he thinks it necessary in the interests of public order (para. 131).

185. I sympathise with the police difficulty in dealing with objects which may be used as offensive weapons but I think it would be unwise to give the police power to direct that such articles should not be carried or worn (para. 132).

186. I reject the proposal that National Front demonstrations should be banned; and also proposals for specific legal provisions to deal with, first, police interference with journalists and photographers, and second, police misuse of truncheons (paras. 134 (1), (2) and (3)).

187. I agree with the proposal that Local Acts should be

brought into line with the Public Order Act (as amended) (para. 134 (4)).

188. I reject a proposal that there should be available a judicial review of any decision to ban or impose conditions on a demonstration (para. 134(5)).

189. In my view it is unnecessary to enact a positive right to demonstrate except as part of a general codification of the law (para. 134 (6)).

190. I agree that public meeting-places should be provided in towns and cities (para. 134 (7)).

191. I reject the proposal that the police should have the power to cancel one demonstration where two opposing parties are planning to march in the same area. Present police powers are sufficient (para. 134 (8)).

192. I strongly recommend the early introduction of an effective independent element into the procedure for the investigation of complaints (para. 134 (9)).

193. On such evidence as I have seen there may well be good reason to wonder whether magistrates do always appreciate the gravity of a breach of public order (para. 150).

194. There are also lessons for demonstrators; above all the need to co-operate with the police. If they do not do so they have only themselves to blame if the law becomes more restrictive (paras. 151—5).

(b) Policing

195. I recommend that the police should confirm the route of a demonstration in writing, in suitable cases – while making it clear that the route might have to be changed in the course of the demonstration, if necessary (para. 130).

196. Consideration should be given to the publication of a pamphlet under a title such as 'Ways and means of co-operation between demonstrators and police' (para. 138).

197. In the light of the events of 15 June police would be wise not to allow a future counter-demonstration to come so close to the object of its opposition. The statutory powers should be used where necessary (paras. 139–40).

198. In dispersing a crowd the police should take care, as far as is possible in the circumstances, to ensure that it does

not have the opportunity to attack at another vulnerable point. Police at the front of a crowd should do what they can to ensure that it has sufficient means of moving away before taking action against it. Police at the rear of a crowd should bear in mind that their action may be of critical importance. These points should be incorporated in police training (para. 141).

199. Warnings should be given before taking action against a static crowd; only exceptionally should no warning be given (para. 142).

200. I reject suggestions that the mounted police and the Special Patrol Group should be withdrawn from duty in relation to demonstrations (paras 143–6).

201. The 'aftermath' situation presents particular problems for police officers in terms of control. A high standard of discipline and control is required of police at this stage. Only so much force and only so many officers should be used in making arrests as are necessary in the circumstances (para. 148).

202. It is important for the police to conduct an effective debriefing when reports of the drawing and use of truncheons, violent incidents and other matters should be made. Senior officers need to develop a continuing capacity for learning from public order operations (para. 149).

COSTS

203. I recommend that the costs, as taxed or agreed, of the parties represented at the Inquiry be paid out of public funds. I was greatly assisted throughout the Inquiry by the counsel and solicitors instructed, all of whom served well not only the interests of their clients but also the public interest.

CONCLUSION

204. Finally, I wish to express my gratitude and admiration for the services rendered to the Inquiry by Counsel for the Inquiry, the Treasury Solicitor and the members of his

staff who acted for the Inquiry, and Mr David Belfall, the Secretary of the Inquiry. The staff of the Treasury Solicitor brought an unrivalled experience and great skill to bear on the task of assembling the mass of evidence and documents necessary to my task. To Counsel for the Inquiry, and particularly to their leader, I am greatly indebted for a fair, but probing, presentation of the evidence and an invaluable review of the evidence at the conclusion of the hearings. Mr Belfall was my indispensable helper and friend throughout all stages of the Inquiry: I would wish to make a special mention of his sustained and shrewd contribution to the preparation of the report. Last, but by no means least, I wish to pay my tribute to the unnamed but devoted civil servants without whose work in the office and at the typewriter the report could never have been written.

205. I take leave of Red Lion Square with a quotation from the evidence of Miss Cathryn Sykes, a school-teacher, who watched from a rooftop the disorders in the square. Asked if it was her impression that the police left it a long time before they started using the horses, she replied,

'Yes. We wondered why they did not bring the horses in earlier: we thought they should have done because the foot police were taking an awful battering.'

And, asked if she thought the police were dealing with the thing calmly, she replied:

'Yes, we thought very well.'

Her assessment of the provocation to which the police in the square were subjected and the quality of their response may stand as the final word. It is the key to a proper understanding of the disorders.

D J BELFALL
(*Secretary*)

LESLIE SCARMAN

7 February 1975

8
A Sufficiency of Seed on Fertile Ground*

This event always reminds me of the Parable of the Sower, with which I am sure you are all familiar. I mean, of course, that the College is the Sower and that those of you who have enjoyed its facilities are the seed. Some of you will perhaps fall by the wayside or on stony ground and I must say that I have known those in the past for whom that fate was entirely appropriate if insufficiently speedy. Some of you will afford the police service the solid commonsense and unremarkable but devoted support on which it basically depends to solve the thorny problems it continually faces. But there are some here who will be destined to play an important part in the next decade or so in the development of the police service, in the preservation and improvement of its standards and performance and in the enhancement of its status and ideals.

There never was a time at which the police were so important to the stability and happiness of our society or when they were more in need of the ability to think for themselves about the part they play in it. For over a century we have been an artisan service trained to uphold a social system but not to think too much about it whilst doing so. The establishment of this College a quarter of a century ago was an indication of the inevitable change in our role. The gradually enlightening and liberating effect of the College is a particular cause for

* Address given at the National Police College, Bramshill, in August 1975.

gratitude for the foresight of those who established it. It is already one of the most important police institutions in Great Britain and will one day, I think, play an even greater part in police affairs.

The very nature of our role in a society which is better equipped to think for itself, to question custom and precedent, to demand greater equality of opportunity and above all to ask of those who govern it the question 'Why?' requires that we ourselves should exercise the same curiosity about our role and the motives and justification for what we do. Sensitive as we certainly should be to judicial rules and procedures to ensure fair trial, to our obligations to democratically constituted police authorities, to the right of privacy of those with whom we deal, we should not be so insensitive as not to consider carefully and curiously the social values to which we subscribe and which we help to maintain. We who alone see the reality and the whole of recorded crime should not be reluctant to speak about it. We who are the anvil on which society beats out the problems and abrasions of social inequality, racial prejudice, weak laws and ineffective legislation should not be inhibited from expressing our views, whether critical or constructive. For we have a personal responsibility in carrying out our duty to enforce and uphold the law. We who have been trained for decades to an unquestioning and unjustified complacency about our system of justice should not regard it as our duty to remain silent about its shortcomings so long as we speak with moderation, with logic and from experience; not so that our point of view on any subject should prevail, but that everyone should be better informed.

The innumerable problems which confront the police service today are capable of definition, given the necessary moral courage and willingness. They may not always be capable of solution but at least they are likely to be more easily bearable if better and more widely understood. Time will only allow me to mention the more obvious ones today, for which you and your guests should both be thankful.

An admirable administrative system of forty-three forces, for example, allows continuance of the longstanding partnership between police, government and local authorities which I believe to be invaluable, but its effectiveness is seriously impaired by a distribution of available manpower which is demonstrably absurd, an absurdity from which the police as as much as successive governments are responsible, but about which official comment has, until recently, been evasive or positively misleading.

The ability to maintain a satisfactory standard of public order in its widest sense is impaired less by an occasionally pusillanimous police force, as a distinguished judge once described the Met., than by pusillanimous laws and pusillanimous courts. The police, at least in central London, no matter how energetic in dealing with unlawful squatting and violence at demonstrations, trade disputes, football matches and in sensitive areas of social deprivation, are hardly likely these days to feel confident of any meaningful assistance from anyone in our difficult and dangerous task. We are sure of a great deal of lip service, but not much else.

Almost 3,000 Metropolitan policemen were assaulted in 1974, 12 per cent more than in 1973. In fact, every three days two go sick after being assaulted, and some remain off duty for lengthy periods. Six were badly injured in a recent ten-day period – three of them stabbed and one knocked unconscious. The average fine of those convicted is far from adequate justification for the attendance at court of even one of the three uniformed policemen, all that we have for each square mile of the Metropolitan Police District which suffers 150 burglaries and 350 autocrimes daily. Without being unnecessarily critical or cynical, someone must point out to the public and even perhaps to the courts that there is a relationship between these unpalatable facts and since no one else is aware of them it is our job to do so. Indeed it is a serious neglect of duty to the service, to society and even to the courts if we do not.

All thinking policemen and women, and presumably all of you here fall within that definition, should welcome the proposal to introduce an independent element into the police complaints procedure to ensure fair treatment for the complainant and the police without weakening the effectiveness of justice or discipline. But once it has been established we must surely go on to demand similar machinery for the examination of complaints against the others involved in the judicial process, the legal profession, the jury and the administration of justice itself. For too long have we been dominated by the false assumption that dubious and blatantly perverse acquittals should not be subject to scrutiny no less close than that given to questionable convictions, since, though rightly, the number of the former greatly exceeds that of the latter.

The purpose of public comment by police ought not to be to provoke hysteria or to argue an increase in our numbers or powers. Far from it. The purpose should be to allow our problems to be seen for the first time in a coherent form so that improvements or solutions can be sought calmly, and logically from evidence, not from speculation or ignorance. This in itself is likely to obviate over-reaction to superficially grave problems. Nothing could be sillier or more irresponsible, for example, than to suggest in public that in the foreseeable future the police are likely to be armed as a routine measure. There has never been less likelihood or justification for such a proposal, not least because of the ready availability of firearms and military assistance for serious emergencies, and to air such a proposal without evidence or logic merely plays into the hands of those who seek to undermine democratic institutions and government by implying a willingness on their part to use arbitrary force. It ignores also the simple truth that this is a proposal with which the overwhelming majority of policemen would probably refuse to comply.

The College seems to me to be the ideal centre for thought, research and discussion about matters of this kind because nowhere else in Great Britain is there available a combination of both practical and academic experience concentrated upon those matters with which the police are concerned. Some valuable work is done at a number of universities, notably at the Institute of Criminology at Cambridge. But most academic research undertaken at universities into crime and the criminal law has little to do with reality and the practical problems confronting the police. A classic example of this is the recent study on juries by the Oxford Penal Research Unit which drew a number of questionable conclusions from trials with a shadow jury. Academic exercises involving 'shadow' juries would be laughable if they were not so sadly misleading and thus positively harmful. How can one assess jury trials in London without considering the actual composition of the jury, after the exercise of the right to challenge, the infinite variety and dubiety of defence tactics, of threats to witnesses, of the awareness and anxiety of learned judges, counsel, Home Office officials and the police about the safety of the increasing number of criminals willing to give evidence for the Crown. There is no mention of these major problems in the various academic papers on jury trials, notwithstanding that the safety of prosecution witnesses and their relatives now constitutes one of the most serious problems in some recent criminal trials. Nowhere other than in the debate on majority verdicts have I seen an admission that some acquittals may be achieved by fear, by intimidation or by malpractice. They are attributed instead by the unworldly or prejudiced academic to the inadequacy of the prosecution or the skill of the defence. Somehow or other we must find means to bring to public notice the sordid reality which can and does mar the criminal process in London of which the academic seems totally unaware. We must find ways of exposing to impartial analysis the too frequent malfunction of criminal justice in a way which does not expose us to suspicion of prejudice, of a desire to convict the innocent, or of an unawareness or unwillingness to accept the need for proper safeguards for the defence. The best way to achieve that objective is by impartial research such as that now being undertaken by Professor Borrie at the Institute of Judicial Administration of the University of Birmingham with the active support of the Home Office. It is sad indeed that, of all those concerned with the administration of justice, the Bar alone has declined to take part, though Dr Samuel Johnson would hardly have been surprised. Research of that kind must be fed by facts and by truth, but it need not and should not be confined to Birmingham. This College is ideally qualified to participate in and to initiate original research and thus to enhance its status and widen its influence upon police affairs and the administration of justice. If the College is to attain the status necessary for the enhancement of the police service it must now aspire to become 'a place of light, of liberty, of learning', Disraeli's definition of a university, as those of you engaged in liberal studies here will recall, and not just a place which police officers must attend in order to qualify for promotion.

I have no doubt that those of you completing your courses today will have enjoyed your time here and will be looking forward to returning to your parent forces. Some of you have long to serve. Do not, I beg of you, under the pressure of your operational duties, forget the College, the purposes that it serves and the purposes it could serve. I will refrain from quoting John McCrae because my hands are not yet failing, as far as I know, but it is to you, rather than to we of a fading generation of policemen, that the College and the service must look for the fulfilment of its aspirations. A sufficiency of seed on fertile ground is its best hope for the future. Let us hope that in some of you it has taken root.

Appendix: Relations with the News Media

General Memorandum Issued 24 May 1973

1. There is no doubt that the operational effectiveness of the force is to a very large extent dependent upon the goodwill, co-operation and support of members of the general public. There are two main ways in which public backing can be obtained or strengthened. The first is obviously by the adoption of a courteous and helpful attitude at all possible times by every member of the force. The second, equally important, is by means of publicity given to the activities of the force in the press and on television and radio.

2. Most members of the public come into direct contact with policemen infrequently and it follows that their image of and attitude towards the force, when not dictated by hearsay, is largely governed by the approach adopted by the news media. It is therefore of the utmost importance that every effort should be made to develop and maintain good relations with news media representatives in order to render it the more likely that their coverage of police activities will be full and fair. Furthermore, if the force as a public service is to be properly accountable for its actions the public has the right to the fullest possible knowledge of its activities.

3. In view of the fact that police sources supply a very large amount of important and interesting news material to the press, television and radio, it would seem that the maintenance of good relations should present no particular problem. Of course, the force has to face certain restrictions on the disclosure of information which stand in the way of

establishing a better relationship with the press. The most important of these restrictions arise from the judicial process, in both criminal and disciplinary cases; the special position of the Metropolitan Police in relation to the Home Secretary as police authority, affecting the discussion of policy matters; the obligation to conform to common policies agreed by chief constables with the Home Office; the need to maintain a substantial degree of uniformity of policy throughout the Metropolitan Police District; the requirement to be as fair as possible to all the news media; the need to observe the individual's right to privacy; and the paramount need to put the public interest before that of either the force or the press.

4. However, relations with the news media are not as good as they could be; there is in particular a reluctance to accept that the role of the news media is to obtain and disclose to the public as much information as possible and that in pursuance of this role they are of course properly concerned with the affairs of the Metropolitan Police. The police have made unnecessary difficulties for themselves by tending to withhold information which could safely be made public, and the flow of information to the Press Bureau at Scotland Yard has not been sufficient to enable the Bureau to serve effectively the force and the news media. This tendency has been encouraged because at times openness with the news media has resulted in incorrect or unfairly critical reporting to which the natural reaction is to be less forthcoming in the future. But I have no doubt that it is in the interests of the force to seek a better working relationship with the press, television and radio. It is my firm belief that the Metropolitan Police have a great deal more to be proud of than the public know and that a little more openness with the news media, heightening trust, confidence and co-operation, is all that is required to correct that ignorance. In particular, there is convincing evidence that given an opportunity to do so the press, both as individuals and collectively, will give a great deal of support to the force. I have therefore decided, with the full support of the Deputy and Assistant Commissioners, to introduce various changes in policy and practice

with the aim of bringing about, over a period of time, a better relationship with the news media and consequently a better understanding on their part and that of the public of the force's problems and policies.

DISCLOSURE OF INFORMATION DIRECT TO THE NEWS MEDIA

5. The aim should be to provide for the supply to the news media of factual information within officers' knowledge about incidents at as low a level as possible. Provided an embargo has not been imposed at higher level and disclosure would not compromise judicial processes in either criminal or disciplinary cases, factual information may be so supplied by any officer of the rank of inspector or above, or by any officer of lower rank who has the prior authority of an officer of the rank of inspector or above. It will be for commanders, detective chief superintendents and chief superintendents in charge of sub-divisions to ensure that officers under their command are fully briefed on the levels at which and extent to which factual information may be supplied. Statements on matters of policy, however, must continue to be referred to the senior departmental officers concerned.

6. Where the necessary confidence and trust has developed between the force and the press there may be occasions when senior officers will feel able to talk to reporters on an 'off-the-record' basis, dealing with matters not for public disclosure, explaining reasons for maintaining confidentiality and specifying what might be published at that stage. It will be for commanders to decide at what levels within their areas of responsibility such discretion may be exercised. Whenever there is doubt about the advisability of supplying information to the press the advice of the News Branch or Divisional Press Liaison Officer should be sought or inquiries referred direct to the Press Bureau. When this is done all relevant details should be supplied immediately.

7. In all dealings with the news media a sympathetic and flexible attitude is to be adopted. So far as possible I wish the force to speak for itself and the result will be to place more

authority and responsibility upon all officers. The new approach to dealings with the news media will of course involve risks, disappointments and anxieties; but officers who act and speak in good faith may be assured of my support even if they make errors of judgement when deciding what information to disclose and what to withhold. I fully accept that if the new measures are to succeed in their objective some mistakes will be made in the process.

SUPPLY OF INFORMATION TO THE PRESS BUREAU

8. If the new policy is to succeed the flow of information to the News Branch through the Press Bureau must be increased and speeded up so that all news items which may be of interest to the media can be made available to them at the earliest possible moment. It is equally important that there should be a helpful, prompt and flexible response to requests from the Bureau for information needed to answer inquiries and it should not always be necessary for the divisional commander or the investigating officer in a case to be contacted when the Press Bureau are seeking information to answer inquiries or clarify facts: on many occasions points of fact could be dealt with at a lower level. The Bureau should be told of any reasons why information should not be disclosed or if there are any special reasons why publicity would be helpful. The Bureau, and indeed the News Branch as a whole, cannot operate effectively without the close co-operation and support of all members of the force.

9. If good relations with all the news media are to be established and maintained it is vital that any information given direct to one or more representatives should be passed on immediately to the Press Bureau who will decide whether in fact it should be regarded as exclusive information or whether it can be made generally available. Editors and senior executives of the news media are in general opposed to any kind of 'lobby' system whereby certain reporters are given preferential treatment as regards disclosure of information.

NEW PRESS IDENTIFICATION CARD AND
FACILITIES TO BE MADE AVAILABLE

10. Following a review carried out in conjunction with senior representatives of the news media, it has been decided to introduce a redesigned and reworded press card. The revised card, which will continue to identify the holder and to bear his or her photograph, will be brought into use in the near future. Facsimiles will be provided for display at stations and all officers are to make themselves completely familiar with the form of the card. It is crucial to the success of the altered approach to relations with the news media that in future holders of the press identification card should find it of real value in day-to-day dealings with the Metropolitan Police, carrying a significance which is readily recognised and accepted by all members of the force. To this end the wording of the new card will lay emphasis on the facilities available to news media representatives rather than the penalties which may be invoked in the event of misuse and will declare that holders should be given all reasonable police assistance to perform their duties. The press card will not carry an automatic right of access to the scene of an incident or convey authority to pass police lines since these must remain matters for the judgement of the senior police officer at the scene. However, in normal circumstances card holders are to be provided with all such information and opportunities for access as can be made available.

11. Although special facilities cannot be accorded to non-holders of Metropolitan and City Police press cards, wherever possible I wish the force to endeavour to meet the reasonable needs of bona fide representatives of the news media who are not press card holders but who may have to undertake, from time to time or in an emergency, an assignment in which police assistance is needed, for example at a major incident. However, where regular inquiries are received from non-card holders the matter is to be brought to the attention of the Press Bureau.

LIAISON WITH THE LOCAL PRESS

12. The more open approach to the news media and the increased supply of information, either direct or via the Press Bureau, is intended to apply to all spheres of the press, television and radio – national, regional and local. So far as the local press is concerned, officers in charge of stations have previously been authorised to give representatives of local newspapers items of purely local news which come to their knowledge. As a further step to improve the supply of information the practice which is already widespread whereby a designated officer is responsible for liaison with the local press on a day-to-day basis is to be extended to every station. Commanders or nominated senior officers should hold briefing meetings once or twice a year for all officers so designated at which the Divisional Press Liaison Officer and a senior 'P' Department representative should be present. It would also be helpful if local press reporters could have the opportunity for regular contact, say at weekly or fortnightly intervals, with an officer of chief inspector or inspector rank at their local station. I am sure there is a great deal more news of purely local interest which could be made available without transgressing any of the principles of confidentiality that the force is required to observe. It must be remembered, however, that any items of news which may be of wider interest should also be made generally available via the Press Bureau.

TRAINING

13. The new policy will depend for its success on the growing understanding by police officers at every level of the need for a good relationship with the news media. The achievement of this depends to some extent upon those responsible for training. Basic training should therefore touch on the general concept of the new policy and intermediate and higher training should stress the advantages to be derived from the avoidance of unnecessary secrecy and from the achievement of mutual trust between the force and the news media. A growing confidence, not likely to be impaired by

inevitable occasional criticism of each other, should prove of great benefit to the police and the news media and thus to society itself.

GENERAL

14. Copies of the text of this memorandum are being supplied freely to the news media.

Index